A Parent's
Guide to
Riding
Lessons

A Parent's Guide to Riding Lessons

Everything You Need to Know
to Survive and Thrive
with a Horse-Loving Kid

ELISE GASTON CHAND

Storey Publishing

The mission of Storey Publishing is to serve our customers by
publishing practical information that encourages
personal independence in harmony with the environment.

Edited by Lisa H. Hiley and Deborah Burns
Art direction and book design by Mary Winkelman Velgos
Text production by Liseann Karandisecky

Illustrations by © Koren Shadmi
Author photos by © Brady Morris

Indexed by Nancy D. Wood

Storey Publishing
210 MASS MoCA Way
North Adams, MA 01247
www.storey.com

Printed in the United States by Versa Press
10 9 8 7 6 5 4 3 2 1

Library of Congress Cataloging-in-Publication Data

Chand, Elise Gaston.
 A parent's guide to riding lessons / by Elise Gaston Chand.
    p. cm.
 Includes index.
 ISBN 978-1-60342-447-9 (pbk. : alk. paper)
 1. Junior riders (Horsemanship)—Training of.
 2. Horsemanship. I. Title.
SF310.5.C48 2009
798.2071—dc22
                        2009023712

To Abby, always and forever.

Contents

Introduction

There's nothing like seeing your child's eyes light up with joy at the first warm breath a kind pony snuffles at her small, tentative hand. Or the flush of pleasure on her cheeks when the pony gently accepts an offered carrot. And seeing your child gain confidence on the back of a willing and trustworthy horse, developing her riding skills, learning the fine tenets of proper horsemanship, and spending time in such a healthy, physical activity — well, parents just don't stand a chance!

But as a parent, what are you to do, especially if you don't know much about horses yourself? How do you help your horse-crazy child follow her passion for horses, but do so safely? Horses (even ponies) are very large animals, with minds of their own. Working with them is not all *My Friend Flicka* and *Misty of Chincoteague,* so one way to start is by determining just how "crazy" your child is.

Horse craziness comes in many degrees, from an all-consuming, almost visceral passion for horses to a more relaxed, but still powerful, desire to be with them. This is not to say that a child's interest in horses must be all-consuming for it to be sincere. There are many rewarding ways to be involved with horses, from casual pleasure riding to intense competition — the key is to find the approach that best suits your child.

Some kids just enjoy horses, like to be around them, and simply want to be able to ride. Other individuals, even at a young age, have a keener interest and long to take regular lessons and participate in horse shows and competitions for the fun of it. And then there are kids who seriously want to become the finest rider possible and to ultimately compete in a specific discipline at the highest levels. Whatever your child's level of interest, the fundamental approach to supporting that interest remains the same: finding knowledgeable, experienced, and skilled guidance so your child can learn in a safe, appropriate way.

How Horse Crazy Is Your Child?

Your child is genuinely "crazy" if she:

- ✪ Draws horses every time a pencil and piece of paper are at hand.
- ✪ Has read every horse book in the library but wants her own copies so she can read them again.
- ✪ Can watch movies about horses over and over and over and over . . .
- ✪ Wants nothing but Breyer model horses for gifts and spends hours playing with them.
- ✪ Frequently uses words that make no sense to you (liver chestnut, withers, cannon bone, piaffe).
- ✪ Urges you to overtake horse trailers on the highway so she can catch a glimpse of any horses inside.
- ✪ Urges you to slow down when you drive past horse farms so she can avidly study the occupants of the fields.
- ✪ Has been caught dressing up the family dog in a close approximation of a bridle, saddle pad, and saddle.
- ✪ Frequently pretends her bike is a horse.
- ✪ Can imitate equine neighs, snorts, and squeals with surprising realism and is often seen pawing at the ground, stamping her foot, and tossing her "mane."

Before going any further with the exploration of the horse world, you need to get an idea of just how determined your child is in her love of horses. The *idea* of horses is lovely, exciting, and romantic, and so, for a true horse-lover, is the *reality* of horses, which often involves hard, physical effort under sometimes unpleasant weather conditions.

In fantasies, the horse is always eager to please, ready to dash off at the slightest touch of a rider's leg, swift and sure and intelligent. In reality, horses have bad days just like people do. They sometimes resent an inexperienced rider tugging at their mouths, plopping down hard on their backs, or digging sharp heels into their ribs. When the weather is hot, they may feel sluggish and want to be back with their friends in the paddock. When the weather is cold, they may feel fresh and spirited and want to run and buck and play.

Questions for Parents to Ask Their Children

The main issue is, will your child still find horses appealing when faced with less-than-perfect reality? To help you find answers in this endeavor, here are some questions to go through with your child.

Why do you want to ride? What kind of riding do you want to do? Do you want to go fast? Do you want to jump? Do you want to look beautiful? Do you want to ride across country? Do you want to chase cows?

How hard are you willing to work in order to ride? Working and caring for horses is physical, it's demanding, it's tiring, and it can be frustrating. Riding is also a privilege — it's expensive and time-consuming. Earning that privilege is important, whether by doing well in school, doing chores at home, or some other effort. Are you willing to put in that effort?

How often do you want to ride? Are you interested in one or two lessons a week? Or do you hope to ride every day? If your scheduled lesson interferes with going to a friend's house or your favorite activity, what would you do?

Will you be a dedicated rider or a fair-weather rider? Will you want to ride when it's cold and windy? Will you want to ride when it's blistering hot outside and the ring is dusty? Do you accept that riding isn't all prancing around on a beautiful steed and that you will have to learn the basics of caring for and handling a horse? If you arrive at the barn to find a mud-caked horse, are you willing to put in the time and effort to clean him up before riding?

How well will you listen to an instructor? Are you willing to do the same thing over and over again until you get it right, even when you feel frustrated or upset? Will you stick with riding even when your muscles are sore and your bottom hurts?

Are you willing to always follow safety precautions? That means wearing a helmet and boots, even if some of the other kids aren't. Does the idea of falling off a horse frighten you? Or do you believe that it's just part of learning to ride?

Questions for Children to Ask Their Parents

Lest you think that a commitment to riding lessons falls solely on your child, here are some questions for your child to ask you as well.

Why are you considering letting me ride? Have you ever ridden and, if so, what was your experience? Do you like horses? Are you afraid of them?

How hard are you willing to work? Are you willing to stick to a schedule and to sometimes reorganize other plans in order to let me ride? If I don't feel like going to a lesson, will you let me off the hook or will you insist that I honor my commitment? If you can't always take me to my riding lessons, how will I get there? Will you mind my muddy boots in your car?

Are you prepared for the financial commitment?

Are you prepared for the emotional commitment? Does the idea of my someday falling off a horse terrify you? Or do you believe that it's just part of learning to ride? If I do fall, will you be okay allowing me to keep going?

How well will you listen to an instructor? Will you watch my lessons and participate in my learning? If I ask you *not* to watch a lesson, will you be offended? Will you watch over my learning to ensure that safety is the primary focus and that the instructor is not rushing me to higher levels when I'm still struggling with the basics? If I participate in competition, will you go to the horse shows and learn proper show etiquette for parents?

After you and your child have a frank discussion of these questions, read on. And take heart — the wonderful gift of riding is something that will stay with your child forever.

A Note About Terminology

We have chosen to use "she/her" when referring to riders and trainers and "he/him" when referring to horses. This is partly in order to avoid the awkwardness of using "he/she" throughout the book and partly a reflection of the general gender breakdown in the field of horseback riding. For whatever reason, horses and girls just seem to go together!

1

What You Need to Know

When confronted with a child's fervent love of horses, some parents may find themselves remembering their own childhood love for horses and endless hours of doodling, reading horse books, or even pretending to be a horse. Non-horsey parents, however, may be unsure how to respond to this inexplicable passion — some may have the first impulse to firmly say "no," while fervently hoping that the interest will quickly pass. Others will wish to be encouraging, without knowing quite how to go about it. In either case, parents wonder about the cost involved, the time commitment, and the safety risks.

Whatever your own response, know that you're not the first parent to feel what you're feeling. The good news is that there are lots of wonderful resources available to you — and your child — to help explore this interest safely, knowledgeably, but most important, *together*.

Talking the Talk

Hands. Describes how the rider holds the reins; "hard hands" hold the reins too short and tight, while "soft hands" maintain a gentle, even contact with the horse's mouth.

Seat. This is the rider's position in the saddle; a "deep" and "balanced" seat is highly desirable, as it means the rider is in good contact with the saddle and, by extension, the horse.

Tack. The equipment used for riding a horse; specifically, the bridle, saddle, girth, and saddle pad.

Tacking up. Putting the riding equipment on a horse, preparatory to riding.

English and Western Riding

Learning to ride a horse involves a great deal more than just sitting in a saddle and letting the horse do all the work. The focus is on the relationship between the horse and rider, of course, but it's also about what the horse and rider are *doing* together. Many experienced riders enjoy pleasure riding or hacking — being on a horse for the sheer joy of it, not working toward any goals, not trying to accomplish anything, just enjoying the experience for its own sake. They may ride in a ring or go out on trails, usually with friends, to enjoy beautiful scenery and variable terrain.

Other riders spend hours working toward specific goals within a particular discipline. The two main styles of riding are English and Western, each with its particular equipment and way of sitting on a horse. Within each style, riders can choose from a number of disciplines, as described below. Some disciplines, such as pleasure or trail riding, can be enjoyed by either English or Western riders. Both styles of riding require a secure seat, good horsemanship skills, and confidence. In any discipline, even the finest riders will say that they are always learning and the horse is their best teacher.

At its best, Western riding teaches the skills of the cowboy, the vaquero, the charro — riders who had to get a hard day's work done from the saddle.

More about Western Riding

While English riding arose primarily from the cavalry tradition, Western riding was developed for hardworking cowboys who spent many hours in the saddle and needed to be able to perform a number of functions (herding livestock, roping animals, fixing fences, and so on) while on horseback. The clothes and tack used in Western riding reflect that need for safety, comfort, and practicality while on the job. Not all Western riders are cowboys, of course! Western disciplines include reining (similar to dressage), barrel racing, and team penning, among others.

More about English Riding

English riding is quite different from Western riding, with the most obvious visual differences being the riders' clothes and the horses' tack (saddle, bridle, and so forth). Many people consider English-style riding more difficult to learn than Western primarily because it requires greater balance in a smaller saddle, without the support offered by the larger Western saddle that has a horn (handle) in front. At more advanced skill levels, however, both styles focus heavily on the rapport between horse and rider to achieve specific goals, whether it be jumping a series of fences or separating a particular cow from the herd.

English riding, which includes activities such as show jumping, classical dressage, and three-phase eventing, is practiced throughout the world. It combines the earliest horse-training and riding traditions, which were developed by cavalry units and nobility over the centuries, with theories from the world's finest horsemen, going back through all of recorded history to perhaps the earliest known, Xenophon the Greek (431–355 BCE).

Individuals who pursue English riding at the highest levels view it as a true art, to be studied and perfected through a lifetime of dedicated effort.

The discipline's foundation in mounted combat training, is particularly evident in dressage, a formal discipline that dates back to the Greeks and Romans. Examples of these combat moves include the pirouette (a spin on the haunches to the left or right) to quickly evade an enemy's sword thrust and the capriole (in which the horse leaps straight into the air and lashes out with his hind legs), which was used against foot soldiers and to unhorse enemy riders. These advanced maneuvers are seen only at the highest levels.

Some Basic Equine Information

Horses are naturally social animals and feel most comfortable and relaxed when surrounded by other horses. They can also find comfort in being handled by an experienced and confident rider, as their natural tendency is to follow and obey a respected leader. In the wild, the herd leader (usually a mare) watches over the herd, warns of danger, leads them to water and good grazing, and keeps discipline and order.

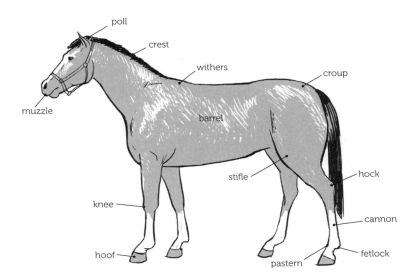

How Many Hands?

Horses are measured in units called "hands." The measurement for height is taken from the point of the withers (where the horse's neck meets his back; that is, the top of the shoulder blades) to the ground. One hand equals four inches (10 cm).

To understand how this works, here are some sample conversions:

12 hands: 12 × 4 = 48 inches (122 cm) or 4 feet (1.2 m) at the withers

16.2 hands: 16.2 × 4 = 64.8 inches (165 cm) or 5 feet, 4 inches (1.6 m) at the withers

Remember that the horse's or pony's head reaches much higher than the withers!

There is a firm line, however, between responsible leadership and harsh treatment, and the two should never be confused. A good leader knows the difference and understands that pain and fear never take the place of respect and understanding.

It may seem odd that an animal as large as the horse would allow comparably small humans to control it so thoroughly, yet this partnership has existed for centuries. What allows us to handle horses is their psychology — a strong herd instinct and the related recognition of pecking order with the natural deference to a leader.

Consistent training helps to reinforce the horse's recognition of the rider as its leader, but even the best training can be defeated by survival instincts such as the "fight or flight" instinct of all prey animals. Understanding just how far training can take you with a horse — when instincts will supersede all training and how to respond appropriately and safely — is the study of a lifetime.

"Horse" Spoken Here

Because horses obviously cannot speak "human," it's imperative that humans learn to speak "horse." Even if you never plan to ride a horse, your understanding and enjoyment of your child's experience will be greatly enhanced if you become familiar with the basics of equine "language." Most equine communication is nonverbal; that is, horses tell one another (and us) a great deal by the way they move and hold their bodies.

The Expressive Ears

Horses can point their ears in all directions and can move them independently of each other, which allows for a variety of expressions. For example, a horse whose **ears are held loose and relaxed,** as in the top drawing, facing somewhat sideways out from his head, is happy and relaxed.

Ears that are up and facing gently forward signal that the horse is alert and happy.

Ears that point slightly back but appear soft and relaxed indicate that the horse is paying attention to something behind him — your child on his back, for instance. The horse is calm and attentive, doing his job pleasantly. If the horse periodically moves the ears backward more, he may be protesting the rider's signals — for example, expressing unhappiness with hands that are holding the reins too tightly (which can make the bit uncomfortable or even painful) or simply grumping about being asked to work when he would rather go back to his friends.

Ears that are pointed hard forward express extreme interest, tension, or even fear, particularly if the horse's head is held high, his neck muscles are visible, and his body appears tense.

Ears that are pinned backward so that they almost touch the horse's neck or disappear into his mane mean that the horse is seriously angry. This is an expression of threat and aggression, which may arise from fear (the flip side of "flight" is "fight").

Ears that flick back and forth quickly, especially if the head is held high, along with the whites of the eyes showing, and the horse possibly snorting loudly through his nostrils, indicates that the horse is very worried about something. A horse giving these signals might decide to bolt quickly and suddenly.

The Mobile Muzzle

Because horses don't have hands, they experience the world most intimately through their flexible and sensitive lips and muzzle. This is especially true of foals, who can often be described as "mouthy." Such exploration is well intentioned and should not be confused with biting or grabbing. For an inexperienced horse person, it can be difficult to determine if the horse is being overly friendly or is looking to nip.

A horse who makes chewing motions, especially in combination with licking his lips, is expressing good intentions and friendliness.

A horse who bares his teeth and/ or snaps, however, is showing extreme aggression — either because he is enraged or because he is terrified.

A horse who scrunches up his top lip and appears to be grimacing is exhibiting the "flehmen response." Horses, especially males, often do this when they smell something particularly interesting, like certain scents or pheromones.

FROM A HORSE-CRAZY KID

I've always loved horses. Horses make me happy — just being on my pony and being close. Thinking of my pony, Little Bit, makes me smile all through my day, because she always loves to be with me. I show my pony I love her just by being close to her and hugging her. All of the other ponies in the world love to bite and kick, but not Little Bit. She is the sweetest pony ever.

I know my pony loves me when she comes close to me and stands so I can put her halter on. And when she comes to me fast when I call her. When I go into her stall, she always comes and stands close to me, with her head against my chest. And I know she loves me because she lets me hug her and she always listens to me and minds her manners.

I will always have horses in my life. I'll have kids and get horses for my kids. I will own a farm and a lot of people will board their horses there in my barn. I want to always have horses to take care of.

— *Abby*, age 5

The Physical Stance

It may seem unlikely, but the way a horse stands can tell you a lot about how he's feeling. You often see **a horse standing with one hind foot cocked** so that the front of the hoof (the toe) is resting on the ground; this indicates that the animal is relaxed and comfortable with his surroundings.

A horse who stands with his head elevated and his body tense is either very excited or is worried about something he sees, hears, or smells. If the former, he may begin to dance around in excitement; if the latter, he's trying to make a fast decision about what it is and how to react to it (flight or fight).

A horse who turns his rear end toward a person is expressing anger and threat — stay away! A horse who hitches his hip while lifting a foot from the ground is threatening to kick — watch out. If, however, the horse uses that hind leg to rub the underside of his own belly, he's simply rubbing off flies or gnats that are tickling him there, and he means no harm to anyone . . . except the insects!

The Telling Tail

You already know that horses use their tails to swish away flies and other insects that can make them miserable. A lazily swishing tail is also the horse's way of showing relaxation and general satisfaction with the world.

Sometimes a horse will lash its tail while he's being worked or ridden. Like the briefly turned-back ears, a quick tail-lash is the horse's way of protesting. It's almost always a very mild form of protest and is just the horse saying, "Look, I'll do what you just asked me to do, but I'd really rather be back in the field with my buddies."

A horse who repeatedly lashes his tail with great urgency (especially if he also has his ears pinned, his head elevated, and is showing the whites of his eyes) is expressing extreme agitation — and anything could be causing the problem. Sometimes, it's a particularly determined biting insect (many of which have very painful bites and draw blood). Sometimes, it's a harsh bit or something painful under the saddle pad (like a sharp thorn) that's causing the horse distress. And, sometimes, the horse is angry and flat-out does not want to do anything the rider or handler is asking of him.

Equine Sounds and Vocalizations

Although body language is paramount, horses do communicate with a variety of sounds. A bugling *neigh* is the horse's way of calling out to other horses. A stallion neighs to tell the mares, "I'm here, ladies!" Horses also neigh to call to a buddy who is out of sight or to figure out where the herd is.

A *whicker*, deep in the horse's chest, is an expression of happiness. Horses use this sound to welcome a good human friend, a mare uses it to comfort her baby, and a barn full of horses make this sound at feeding time to welcome the person who feeds them.

Occasionally you will hear horses make a short, high-pitched, squealing sound at one another. This lets other horses know that they've had enough of the other horse's attentions — most often, this occurs during initial meetings between two strange horses. And a mare will squeal at a stallion to flirt with him. We may find it strange, but stallions love it!

A horse will make a loud, high-pitched blowing sound through dilated nostrils when he is highly aroused — perhaps in extreme excitement upon seeing a new horse walking toward the herd or in severe agitation upon sensing a possible threat. This blowing sound is often accompanied by high head and tail carriage, tense body posture, and lots of prancing around.

Learn from the "Expert"

It's a rare thing for a child to be the most knowledgeable person in the family. Yet that is probably the case in your own household when the topic is horses. What a wonderful gift you can give your child, therefore, by "talking horses" with her and allowing her to share her knowledge with you and to teach you some of what she knows about her favorite topic. A great way to do this is to have her quiz you: "What's a bay? Where does the bridle go? What do you call a female horse?" It's okay — preferable, actually — that you not have all the answers to her questions. The joy is twofold — being the teacher and spending time with you.

2

Finding the Right Place to Ride

Your child is no doubt sincerely devoted to the idea of horses, but the reality of them often proves to be another thing. The best way to discover if the passion will last is to sign your child up for a series of riding lessons. Even though many children will beg relentlessly for a pony of their own, that step should be taken only after a great deal of thought and planning, and only after your child has shown an ongoing commitment to learning about horses and learning to ride properly and safely.

There are many different types of facilities that offer riding lessons, and we'll discuss what to look for in this chapter, but the first step is making a connection with an instructor who can take your child through the first few stages of learning.

Talking the Talk

Equestrian center. A professional facility that may have multiple arenas and many well-trained horses. Because centers usually have several trainers on staff, it's possible to learn many disciplines and have the skilled guidance, higher-level horses, and facilities needed for each. Equestrian centers often hold horse shows, exhibitions, and other equestrian-related events.

Lesson barn. A generic term that refers to any facility where riding lessons are given.

Riding school. Combines a dedicated focus on learning to ride well with hands-on instruction in horse care. Riding schools are often owned and operated by the senior instructor and may have an assistant trainer or student trainers on staff. Most riding schools have several "lesson master" horses to accommodate a variety of riding levels and abilities.

Finding a Good Instructor

The first step in finding an instructor is to find out which stables in your area offer riding lessons. Lesson barns come in all shapes and sizes, from an enormous and sprawling professional equestrian center with many trainers on staff to a small, private barn in which the owner gives lessons to a handful of students on two or three horses. It's not the size or grandness of design that's key here, however — you should be looking for safety and knowledge and appropriateness of instruction. And just because people say they give lessons and have gentle horses doesn't mean that they are qualified to teach or that they actually do have appropriate horses for beginners.

There are several ways to do your research. Start with an Internet search, typing in something like "stable AND 'mycity'" (meaning use the name of the location where you live). Try variations too: "riding lessons AND 'mycity'," for example. Some stables, though not all, advertise in the local yellow pages or the local classified weekly papers. Some post business cards and fliers on the bulletin boards in the local feed stores and tack stores. You can try calling horse vets (sometimes listed under "veterinarians, large animal") in your area and asking if any of their clients give riding lessons. And don't forget about the county Extension agents who specialize in horses as well as any local 4-H group(s).

It's also worth asking around your neighborhood and at your child's school to see if anyone can recommend a lesson barn — personal referrals are a great way to locate a barn and a good instructor. Whether armed with a referral or having found a barn through research, you'll want to follow the same process for checking them out for yourself. Just because a barn is right for someone else doesn't mean it will be the right place for your child. You can't always be sure that the barn was thoroughly checked out by the person who gave you the referral; and personalities and teaching styles differ.

Start by calling the stables you've found. Ask to speak with the owner or barn manager if possible; first ask, though, if they have time to talk, since they may have a barn full of kids and horses at that moment. Consider how professional they are in their responses — the person on the phone, whether he or she is the trainer or instructor or barn owner, should be knowledgeable, patient, and interested in your inquiry. You should be aware, however, that a lot of barn phones are answered by the students themselves, so don't be too quick to judge the barn by the person answering the phone!

Asking the Right Questions

The following questions will help you determine if this stable has the right kind of learning situation for your child. If these are answered to your satisfaction, plan a visit to the barn to see what the facilities look like and to observe a lesson before making a commitment.

1. What age riders do you teach?
2. Does your barn specialize in a particular discipline?
3. Do you have experienced and well-mannered lesson horses?
4. What are the instructor's qualifications?
5. What are your safety precautions?
6. How would you define your lesson program?

Let us examine each of these questions more thoroughly.

What Age Riders Do You Teach?

There is a great deal of debate over "how young is too young?" Some instructors will not teach anyone younger than eight years of age. These instructors feel that younger children simply don't have control of their own bodies yet; they lack balance, strength, and coordination, which puts them at greater risk of injury around horses. Other instructors believe that five years of age is acceptable, assuming the proper safety precautions are taken.

Aren't Lessons Expensive?

You don't always get what you pay for: obviously, one of the factors in selecting a lesson barn will be expense. But the lowest price isn't necessarily the best option and the highest doesn't guarantee the best learning experience. The most important element in selecting a lesson barn should be your child's welfare as expressed through the operation's safety efforts, the dependability of the lesson horses, the skill of the instructors, and the condition of their facilities.

A more important issue, however, is your child's own readiness. Is she sincerely interested? Is she mature enough to exercise personal control and not race up to a horse, yelling and jumping up and down? Is she balanced enough to sit quietly in a saddle? And is she intellectually focused enough to take instruction?

If your child meets all of these qualifications, a five-year-old on a dead-calm pony, under the supervision of a skilled and experienced instructor, in a controlled situation and a small enclosure, would be acceptable. Children this age should never, under any circumstances, be allowed loose on a horse, however.

Does Your Barn Specialize in a Particular Discipline?

Truthfully, in the beginning stages of learning to ride, the particular discipline (type of riding, such as dressage, hunt seat, Western pleasure) doesn't really matter. What's critical is for a new rider to develop a solid and proper foundation (good seat, soft hands, knowledge, and confidence). Rather than focusing on a particular discipline, look for a barn that specializes in teaching children to ride and that has well-trained and experienced school horses.

Then why ask this question? It helps you determine how knowledgeable and skilled the instructor is. If the person answers that she rides or teaches every discipline, well, sure, that's possible. But the follow-up question should be, "What's your specialty?" If the person can't specify, you should wonder about this. Generalists do exist in the riding instruction world, but people who are really passionate about riding almost always have a favorite way to ride. That passion will translate itself to their students, so it's useful to know which discipline is of greatest interest to the instructor. You're also trying to establish rapport with the instructor, so asking about her interests is a logical first step.

Do You Have Experienced and Well-Mannered Lesson Horses?

This is critical. A beginning rider needs a calm, experienced lesson horse so that he or she can focus on just learning to ride. Aside from the obvious safety issues, a fractious pony or horse could terrify your budding rider before she ever gets a chance to learn whether riding is something she wants to continue.

"Lesson masters," as these horses are called, are worth their weight in gold because it takes a certain disposition to put up with day after day of inexperienced riders hanging on the reins, thumping their sides, tilting sideways in the saddle, and being clueless or fearful. A good beginner's horse might not be the most beautiful, but he will pack children from sunup 'til sundown in a consistent, trustworthy, and dependable manner.

Sizing Up Horse and Rider

When considering the type of lesson horses at a barn, keep in mind that the mount should fit the physical stature of the rider. Putting a small child on a 16.2-hand horse (about 5½ feet at the withers), no matter how gentle the horse, makes no sense. With such a stretch up, how would an adult standing on the ground properly assist the child in need? Young children should ride small ponies, ideally, 12 to 13 hands in height. Period. That puts the child about four feet from the ground, which is plenty. Most children find it intimidating to be any farther off the ground.

Here's an acceptable way to determine if the rider and the pony/horse fit: With the feet in the proper length stirrups, the bottom of the rider's soles should be about even with the bottom of the animal's belly.

What Are the Instructor's Qualifications?

Intermediate to experienced riders who want to pursue a specific discipline need highly qualified instructors who are certified, who have competed successfully in their chosen discipline, and who have a barn full of experienced and talented horses on which to compete.

Beginning riders, however, have different needs, so look for a barn with an instructor who specializes in teaching beginning riders. This takes a special level of patience, kindness, and the ability to find things that are done well and recognize them enthusiastically rather than harp on what is being done wrong. The beginner's instructor also needs to be creative and engaged in order to find ways to make even the most repetitious lessons fun and interesting.

Some instructors seek certification, just as professionals in other fields do, to enhance their knowledge and professionalism. There are a variety of certifications offered, some online, some from individuals who have created their own training and instruction methods (with varying standards and results), and some through highly reputable associations and training centers. One of the latter is the American Riding Instructors Association (ARIA).

Above all else, the instructor must focus on safety. He or she must insist on the proper gear for the rider and must make sure the horse's tack is in good repair and properly fitted to the individual horse.

The instructor must also be certain the horse is in good health and is behaving appropriately before ever allowing a child on his back. Even lesson masters have bad days! A good instructor won't use a horse who is lame or sore in any way, or who has been used several times already that day.

> Anyone who takes on the responsibility of teaching a potentially dangerous sport to children must have the skills to address these issues, the foresight to prevent problems before they happen, and the motivation to immediately address any issues that crop up.

Professional Memberships

Asking if a barn or an individual instructor is a member of a horsemanship organization gives an opportunity to learn more about their approach to horsemanship and lessons. As in any other profession, organizational involvement can be an additional sign of professional dedication and credibility.

Organizations might include the United States Pony Club (USPC), an outstanding organization focused on teaching horsemanship to children aged six and older; United States Equestrian Federation (USEF), the governing body for American equestrians; or the United States Dressage Federation (USDF), the governing body for the discipline of dressage. There are many, many others, for nearly every breed of horse or style of riding you can imagine.

What Are Your Safety Precautions?

The instructor should be able to provide a lengthy description of how she and the barn's staff go about keeping students safe. Here are some issues that should be covered:

- Do they insist that riders always wear a certified riding helmet? Do they ensure that it's properly fitted?
- Do they regularly clean and inspect tack, making sure it's in good working order and that none of the leather or stitching is rotting or splitting?
- Are the arenas regularly maintained to make sure the footing is safe and even?
- Do the instructors (or trainers or exercise riders) regularly "fine-tune" the lesson horses to reinforce their manners and refresh their training?
- What do they do with horses who misbehave? How do they define "misbehave"? Do any of their horses bite or kick? Do any of them buck or rear?
- What happens if/when a horse does any of these things? (The answer should be an adamant response that the animal is removed permanently from the lesson program.)

Describe Your Lesson Program

Many lesson barns provide a printed brochure or program that describes the levels of lessons offered and exactly what students will learn at each level. Ask for a copy to be sent to you. The following is an example of what you might expect:

Beginning riders will learn the proper names of the horse's main body parts. They will learn to properly groom, lead, and tie a horse, as well as how to tack up (put the equipment on). They will learn how to mount and to sit in the proper position, how to hold the reins, and how to steer and to stop at the walk.

Second-level riders will learn the names of horse colors and breeds. They will learn how to do a sitting trot and a posting trot, including the use of trotting posts or poles (rails laid flat on the ground for the horse to walk or trot over) and the ability to perform controlled movements (circles, serpentines, and so on) around the arena.

Each barn will have different ways of achieving the basic goals. The point is that there be a coherent lesson plan, with goals to work toward that can be measured and achieved.

What's a Show Barn?

From the perspective of identifying the ideal lesson barn for your child, it's helpful to know if the barn is considered a "show barn." Although this should not be the deciding factor in whether you have your child take lessons there — it's just another piece of information to consider — riding at a show barn may entail a commitment to participate in horse shows. Riding at a show barn often means that the students are expected, or even required, to regularly compete in horse shows around the area. Generally, show barns will have a particular discipline (jumping, for example, or reining, or dressage).

Knowing your child and the degree of her interest and dedication will help you to decide if a show barn would be the ideal place for her to learn to ride. For a beginner, a show barn might feel intimidating or it might be inspiring. Show barns can be a great place for intermediate or advanced riders to hone their skills and to gain broader recognition for their efforts and talent in the discipline of their choice.

The Barn Visit

After you finish your phone calls and have a pretty good feeling for two to three barns on your list (if you're fortunate enough to live in an area with several stables), it's time to schedule some barn visits. Ask the instructor if you can observe a lesson that matches your child's skill level. And be sure to spend time just visiting, talking with the instructor between lessons (be prepared for, and patient with, interruptions, as students will be in and out with a real-time need to have their questions answered).

Talk with some of the students and observe how well they seem to get along with one another. Watch how the horses are handled and how the instructor interacts with the students. Note if there are older students helping the younger ones; if so, do they appear confident, attentive, and appropriately knowledgeable? Are they good with younger kids?

There are bound to be other parents waiting for a lesson to end, so use the opportunity to talk with them and see what they think of the barn, of the instructor, of the horses, and so on. Ask them if there have ever been any safety issues or if a rider has ever been injured. See if you can get a sense for whether they're pleased with their child's experience or if they're involved with the barn only because they're not sure where else to go.

Ask to observe a lesson or two at any barn that you are considering. Seeing the instructor in action will give you and your child a much clearer idea of how good a fit that particular establishment will be.

Surveying the Stables

As you're looking around, consider the facilities. While it's important that the buildings and grounds be well maintained and tidy, the primary consideration should be safety. Here are a few things to look out for.

The Aisles. Barn aisles see a lot of traffic, especially between lessons. Are the aisles wide enough to accommodate lots of (big) bodies safely? Is there enough room for students and horses to move around one another? Are the floors uncluttered or are they used for storage of tack trunks, hay, or equipment?

The Stalls. Horses don't need ritzy quarters, but a barn must be basically clean, which means that the aisles should be swept regularly, stalls cleaned out daily, manure disposed of properly. Are the stalls well-bedded and free of the strong smell of ammonia? Of course you'll catch whiffs of ammonia (it's a barn, after all), but your eyes shouldn't be watering or your nostrils burning.

The Rules. Are children allowed to handle the horses without supervision or must they wait for the instructor's okay? Do the children taking lessons and handling horses have on proper clothes (good boots and hard hats)? Are dogs allowed? Many students have younger siblings who tag along to the barn; are they allowed to run loose and be loud?

Public Spaces. How does the office look? Okay, scratch that — barn offices are usually an example of controlled chaos. But check out the tack room — is it clean and organized? Are the saddles and bridles and blankets neatly hung on pegs? Eyeball the equipment — does the leather look clean and solid or is it dirty and cracked? Are the saddle blankets stained and covered in hair? Are the girths or cinches dirty and sweat-stained? Or is everything neat, tidy, and in good order? Remember: if you select this barn, you'll be depending on the equipment you're looking at to keep your child safe and in control of a large animal.

An example of a tidy and well-maintained barn with a 14-foot-wide aisle, which allows plenty of room for horses and people to move about.

The Importance of the Barn Environment

People are people and, just like with any other group, there will be an environment at each barn that reflects the personalities and interests of the people who spend time there.

There's no "right" or "wrong" environment. Some barns are laid-back and relaxed, some are intense and highly focused, and so on. The key is to find a barn that reflects your child's personality, a place where he or she will thrive, will have the opportunity to learn from a skilled and experienced horse person, and will enjoy meeting other kids with similar personalities.

It's important that you are comfortable with the environment too, because chances are good that you'll be spending some time hanging out there as you wait for a lesson to finish or while attending an event.

A Word on the Youngest Riders

If you feel that your five- or six-year-old child is capable of starting lessons and the instructor agrees, be aware that a child that young should never be put on a pony and allowed to be in control of the reins. The proper way to begin teaching very young children is in a round pen (a small, fenced-in area with sandy footing, about 60 feet in diameter).

The pony should be properly tacked up, using either a Western saddle (which has a horn, like a handle, on the front to hold onto) or a lead line saddle (which looks like an English saddle but has a strap or handle on the front to hold onto).

The First Lessons

A qualified and experienced person should lead the pony quietly, calmly, and at the walk only. This is called a "lead line" lesson. It should be private (just your child) and shouldn't last more than 30 minutes, since young children tire easily and have a hard time concentrating for longer periods.

The lessons should focus on helping the child gain confidence in being up so high, learning to sit tall and quietly, keeping his or her feet in the stirrups (not as easy as you'd think), and developing good balance. This may sound tedious to an adult, but to a child, the thrill of just being on a pony is significant. And a good instructor will find ways to keep the lessons interesting — a pole on the ground for the pony to step over can look to a child like a four-foot-tall jump, and the satisfaction of crossing it at a stately walk does wonders for the child's excitement and confidence.

Making Progress

Only when the child can keep her balance, maintain her seat, consistently keep her feet properly in the stirrups, should she be allowed to take up the reins and learn how to hold them properly and (for the sake of keeping the kind pony kind) somewhat loosely. At this point, still on the lead line for safety, the child can be allowed to ask the pony to turn left and right and to stop.

When the child has developed the consistent and confident ability to steer and to stop, the instructor will consider allowing the pony and rider to go into a fenced-in arena. When this transition occurs, it is advisable to begin a series of longe (pronounced "lunge") lessons in which the pony is at the end of a long line with the child mounted and the instructor holding the line and controlling the pony as he circles around. This gives the child a chance to experience riding in a much bigger space at some distance from the instructor before adding the complexity of controlling the pony on her own.

A Word to Parents

When you're the adult tasked with leading a pony around while your child rides and maybe the weather is unpleasant or you've had a long day at work or you're just plain bored with going in circles . . . look over your shoulder at your child's face. Her expression will probably be enough to put a spring in your step and help you make a few more circuits of the round pen or arena.

Assessing the Arenas

While not every facility has an arena, they are especially important for youngsters learning to ride. A fenced arena provides a contained area in which a rider can focus without having to worry about steering around obstacles or having to deal with uneven footing, as you would in a field. What's the weather in your area like? Does it rain a lot? Is the summer sun merciless? A covered or an enclosed arena may be a necessary consideration.

Arenas can range from purely workmanlike to palatial and spectacular. There are three standard types of arenas — indoor, covered, and outdoor — which can be further refined for specialized needs such as jumping, dressage, or Western disciplines such as cutting, reining, roping, or barrel racing. Whatever the type, you'll need to consider the following factors, as the arena should be the sole area in which your child will ride (at least until he or she develops significant riding skills and confidence).

All arenas should be large enough for the disciplines practiced in them, should have smooth footing, and should be lighted so that there are no shadows or overly bright spots cast by the lights, since these could frighten a horse.

Fencing and Footing

What kind of perimeter fencing does the arena have?
Whether indoor or outdoor, the arenas where beginners ride
should be enclosed so the pony or horse can't bolt and run away.
Inexperienced riders need arenas with solid, chest-high (to the
horse) fencing to help control the horse while working in the
arena. An enclosed arena also helps young riders feel a little
more confident.

What is the footing and how deep is it? The footing should
be even (no holes or depressions, nothing that could cause a
horse to stumble) and forgiving (riders do fall). The best footing is sand that's regularly raked by hand or machine. You may
also see shredded rubber or shredded bark. Raw dirt is never a
good choice, as it compacts like concrete when dry, is bad for the
horse's legs and feet, and is dreadful to fall on in the event a rider
loses her seat.

How well does it drain? Slick and sloppy footing after a
rainstorm is unsafe. Although this is more typically an issue in
outdoor arenas, be aware that indoor rings can also have drainage problems. It always pays to ask.

Is the ground level? A stumbling horse can throw off even
the most experienced rider's balance — for an inexperienced
rider, it can mean the difference between staying in the saddle
and falling.

Does the arena become dusty when in use? This can be an
issue either indoors or out, especially with several riders using it.
Dust, especially blowing dust, makes riding extremely unpleasant and can lead to respiratory problems for both the horse and
the rider.

Size and Safety

The arena must be large enough to accommodate the number of horses used in the lesson with at least three horse-lengths between each horse/rider combination. And there should be enough room for everybody to get away from each other if something, somehow, sets off one of the horses. Plus, there must be enough room for more experienced riders to learn how to canter and to safely make it all the way around the arena before having to put on the brakes.

Looking at Lighting

Your child will probably be riding after school or in the evening. Whether the arena is indoor, covered, or outdoor, it's essential that the lighting effectively light the arena. Here are a few factors to consider:

✪ Are there enough lights?

✪ Are they powerful enough?

✪ Are the light poles tall enough? (Your child will be on top of a horse, so you don't want her to be blinded by bright lights on too-short poles; also, in areas with lots of bugs, it's useful to have the lights quite high, since light attracts bugs.)

✪ Are the lights focused well? There shouldn't be any "hot spots" (areas of intense light), dim spots, or shadows, which can look like a frightening hole in the ground to a horse.

✪ Are any of the arena lights burned out?

✪ Where is the light switch? Does the facility owner allow riders to turn them on or off when they wish? (If so, please always be courteous and turn off lights when your child is the last to vacate the arena. Most facilities operate on extremely tight budgets and big electric bills can wreak havoc for them.)

There should never be anything unsafe in the arena — no trash, no stored equipment, nothing a rider could fall on or that a horse could slam into. If the equipment is placed between the arena's rail and the outside wall, it's probably fine. But if it's located someplace that a horse and rider could directly access it, then it creates a hazard. Remember that a frightened horse doesn't pay much attention to what's in front of him when he bolts — he's too busy running away from whatever frightened him. So you cannot count on a spooked horse to avoid hazards in his path, let alone a rider who might become unseated. The key is simple common sense — if there's a possibility that an item could become a hazard, then it *is* a hazard and needs to be moved.

Is There a Round Pen?

Not every facility has a round pen, which is an enclosed circular area for working horses in close proximity, but they are incredibly useful when working with inexperienced children, especially if the children are quite young and have never sat on a horse or pony. Round pens create a much smaller area in which the young student can ride, with the instructor close at hand. Because round pens also tend to focus the horse or pony and to help him keep his attention on the rider and on the instructor, they are often used for training purposes as well.

The ideal size for a round pen is about 60 feet in diameter, which makes a large enough space that the student can control the horse or pony to turn in different directions and to stop but is not enough space for the animal to move at a high rate of speed.

> A good instructor will keep the lesson interesting by frequently having the students change direction, ride in small circles, step over poles, and weave through cones.

Round pens are commonly created with a series of metal-pipe panels but can also be constructed with solid walls. They are usually open to the elements; however, a covered round pen is wonderful in hot climates or inclement weather.

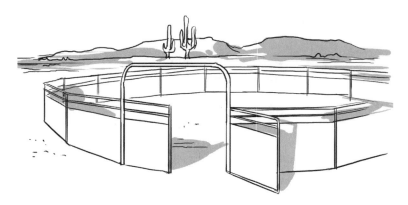

This is a panel-style round pen with solid walls. A round pen should be about 60 feet in diameter and must have proper footing.

Finally, what's true for footing in arenas is also true for round pens — it shouldn't be too deep or too hard, it should be level and shock-absorbing, should drain well, and should be managed to control dust (especially in a solid-wall round pen where airflow is restricted by the design).

The Evaluation Ride

All good instructors will require an evaluation ride to determine the rider's balance and comfort level. If the child has been on a horse before, the instructor will assess her skill level. The number of people of all ages who say they're "experienced riders" is legion, but truly experienced riders are not that common. An experienced rider is competent at judging a horse's abilities and temperament and has the skill to adjust her own riding to handle the animal. "Experienced" does not describe a rider who has frequently sat on a horse doing the nose-to-tail trail ride during summer vacation!

A good instructor will listen politely to the rider's description of her ability and then will personally assess the rider's skills. The instructor often does this by putting the rider up on a trustworthy school horse, then longeing the horse while observing the rider's seat, leg position, balance, and so on. (Longeing is when the horse is put on a long line and moves in a circle around the handler — his speed is controlled by the handler on the ground and not by the rider on his back.)

Only after the initial assessment confirms that the child possesses the appropriate skills should she be allowed to control the horse in the arena under the instructor's supervision. Many

Going to Horse Camp

Riding camps provide a wonderful way for kids to become involved with horses and to help determine their true level of interest. As with other camps (such as soccer or football or cheerleading or band), riding camps typically occur during the summer months when school is out. They can last a few hours several days a week or can be all-day affairs that run for weeks. Many include an overnight component.

All of them involve horses, of course, so must be held at a barn or appropriate facility. The key is to determine the level of involvement with the horses and the intended outcome for each camp — in other words, what should the participants be able to do at the camp's conclusion? What is the camp's lesson program intended to teach?

Just as with any other type of camp, not all are created equal. The worst of them are little more than a day-care situation that just happens to be held at a riding barn, while the best offer superb training from dedicated equestrian professionals, using well-trained horses, in an environment that encourages a love of horses and of learning about them.

Finding the right camp for your child and for your situation requires time, research, and on-site inquiries. You should apply the same criteria to a riding camp as you'd apply to a lesson barn.

beginning riders (even ones who have had some lessons but need more attention to the fundamentals) will continue doing longe lessons until the instructor determines that the rider is skilled enough (and confident enough) to be allowed to control the horse in the arena.

This initial lesson is also an excellent opportunity for you to evaluate the instructor. Pay close attention to everything that goes on. Note how the instructor interacts with your child and how he or she handles the horse or pony. Watch how your child relates to the instructor and your child's demeanor around the horses, as well as when mounted. See how the horse or pony behaves. And, best of all, after the lesson, ask your child how she felt about the lesson, the instructor, the barn, and the horses.

Longeing is a technique used to train horses and to work with inexperienced riders to develop their confidence. It's also a great method for perfecting specific skills, even for more experienced riders, since the person on the ground controls the horse, allowing the rider to concentrate on her own movements.

STILL CRAZY ABOUT HORSES

I have loved horses since as far back as I can remember breathing! Nobody else in my family seemed to have this horse "gene," but it's been with me forever. As a child, horses meant everything to me — the very reason to live. It meant getting excited when we passed them in a pasture as we drove by in the family station wagon, and I couldn't crank my neck far enough around to see them. Or approaching a horse trailer on the highway to see what was inside (which I admit still gives me a thrill!).

I used to spend hours with my best friend crawling around on the front lawn on all fours, pretending we were horses. We would ride our bikes as far as we could go to all of the nearest stables so we could walk the aisles and pet every head that would hang out of the stall to greet us. And we played with our model horses for endless hours.

My parents tried to discourage it, thinking it would be a phase I would grow out of — in fact, my mom is still waiting for that to occur! I think it was hard for them to understand being so passionate about something when they just didn't get it. I think when one is born with the horse bug — completely and totally captivated — it's hard for anyone to understand if they don't have the bug themselves. I didn't get my first horse until I was an adult, but I kept the passion with me all through the years and finally made it a reality when I was 29.

— *Margaret*, age 37

Making a Decision

How do you know when you've hit the jackpot? When you've found the barn that's perfect for your child? When you've found a safe and skilled instructor who's also great with kids?

Well, you made an excellent first step by doing your research. If everything you've seen and heard feels right, and the orientation lesson is a success, *trust your own instincts.* How do you feel about what you've seen and the people you've met? How does your child feel about what she's seen and the people she's met? This is your child and no one knows her better than you do. No one is in a better position to select the right barn and the right instructor than you are.

The Best Barn

Which of the examples below is the perfect barn?

- ✪ A serious facility that is focused entirely on following riding traditions, teaching horsemanship skills, and competing at recognized shows throughout the season.
- ✪ A place that is informal, relaxed, maybe a little disorganized. The horses are all healthy and happy, the children have a lot of fun, and there's usually music playing and people sitting around talking.
- ✪ A palatial facility where the horses live better than some humans do. A staff of instructors teaches several disciplines and there are multiple arenas onsite. The center is run efficiently and is spotless, and there are very clearly defined rules and procedures.
- ✪ A small stable run by the owner, who's also the sole instructor with a talented high school student who helps out. The daily barn work is performed by her, along with the help of several horse-crazy kids who are thrilled by the chance to spend more time with horses.

The answer is: *whichever one feels best to you and your child.*

3

The Ins and Outs of Taking Lessons

In a great many families, both parents work outside the home. Many families have only a single parent. Children are heavily scheduled. Many parents feel that their children's homework load is heavier than it was in their day. Families seem to be constantly moving from one event to another. Adding another event to already packed calendars can seem like insanity.

One way to make sure that homework gets done, that family responsibilities are met, and that chores are completed is to engage your child's sense of fair play and understanding that riding lessons are a privilege and not a right. Maintaining good grades in school and fulfilling personal commitments in order to continue lessons not only help to make the added event doable but also help to set a terrific work ethic and follow-through on commitments that will stay with your child throughout her life.

Once you've found an appropriate lesson barn and made the commitment to a series of lessons, there are some basic rules to follow. You will also have a lot to learn yourself as you watch your child from the rail.

Talking the Talk

Discipline. The two general disciplines of English and Western riding are further divided into particular styles or practices, such as dressage, jumping, reining, and equitation.

Longe (pronounced "lunge"). The handler works the horse from the ground with a long line attached to the bridle, directing him in a large circle.

Proper Safety from Head to Toe

As a parent, your first concern will always be for your child's safety, a topic that is covered throughout this book. The one absolute rule that you should establish with your child before agreeing to any sort of riding program is that she must always wear the proper gear. And the two items of proper gear that are absolutely required are a certified safety helmet and suitable boots.

No Helmet, No Horse

The vast majority of riding helmets available today, from the economical to the wildly expensive, are "ASTM/SEI certified," which means they are approved for equestrian activities. (ASTM/SEI stands for American Standard for Testing Materials and the Safety Equipment Institute.) If it doesn't have that certification, don't even try it on.

Hunt caps, derbies, top hats, cowboy hats, and other styles are not approved for riding and are for appearance only. These kinds of hats do not protect the rider's head in the event of a fall; many of them won't even stay on if the rider hits the ground. *Be aware that even with a helmet on, a hard fall can result in a concussion.* This is because the helmet protects the skull but does not protect the brain from hitting the skull, which is what causes a concussion.

Even a certified riding helmet will do little if it does not fit correctly. Take your child to a local tack shop and ask one of their staff to help you select and fit a certified helmet. Fitting a helmet isn't difficult. Here is what you should look for:

- The helmet should fit all the way down onto the top of the head, cupping the entire skull. If it doesn't, it is too small.
- The edge of the helmet should be no more than 1½ inches above your child's eyebrows.
- Before buckling the chin strap, have your child vigorously shake her head back and forth. If the helmet moves around, try a smaller size.

- Ask your child to gently nod "yes" to make sure that the helmet doesn't slip. Your child's skin can move a little, so that the eyebrows go up and down, but the helmet itself should not move independently. If it does, try a smaller one.
- Buckle the chin strap and adjust it so that it fits comfortably under your child's chin, in the notch between the jaw and the throat. Your child should be able to comfortably drop her chin toward her chest without being garroted, but you should not be able to get more than the width of two fingers, sideways, into the loop of the chin strap.

Riding helmets are now made in light but very durable material, and designs often include ventilation holes so that air can circulate and keep the rider's head cooler. Sun visor extensions can be attached to the helmet to provide additional protection from glare. In the winter, ear covers protect exposed ears from freezing winds.

And helmets are no longer offered in only traditional black velvet or velveteen — many models are decorated with wild colors and patterns. Any helmet can be made downright eccentric, given the delightful choices available in nylon hat covers, which are easily changed to suit your child's taste.

Buy Good Boots

Proper riding boots have a heel of about one inch and a sole that is neither too grippy nor too slick. The purpose of the heel is to prevent the rider's foot from slipping through the stirrup and becoming caught — if the horse panicked and the rider fell off, the rider would be dragged (a nightmare scenario for anyone). The surface of the sole affects the rider's ability to safely keep her foot in the stirrup without slipping out or getting stuck.

The boot's structure from side-to-side is also critical — should the horse fall and the rider's foot become trapped underneath, the strength of the sole could prevent the rider's foot from becoming crushed by the horse's weight. (Another nightmare scenario — but be assured that accidents like this are uncommon.) Finally, the toebox on good riding boots protects the rider's foot from injury if a horse steps on it ("when" is more accurate — everybody gets stepped on sometime!). You really don't want your child to be wearing sneakers or flip-flops when that happens.

> Although kids do fall off horses in lessons, it is rare for them to sustain serious injuries in a safe and well-managed riding program.

For English riding, short boots (also called paddock or jodhpur boots) are appropriate for young children. They are often worn with jodhpurs or breeches that pad the inside of the leg so the stirrup leathers don't pinch. They can also be worn with jeans, in which case half chaps to protect the leg are a good idea. They are available in both laced and zippered styles.

Paddock boots are fine for Western riding also, though cowboy boots are more traditional. Look for the "roper" style, which has a rounded toe and is more comfortable than narrow-toed models. In any type of boot, your child should be able to flex his or her foot easily so she can position it properly in the stirrup (heel down, toe up).

The boots should fit well and be comfortable — there's nothing like the special agony of boots that rub heels raw and cause blisters. The boots should be just as comfortable worn in the saddle as they are while she is walking around.

Note: While artificial materials are cheaper, they do not allow the foot to breathe — especially important in hot climates. Invest a little extra and get real leather uppers.

Basic Lesson Attire

Riding clothes have been designed over hundreds of years to serve specific, functional, and sometimes, safety-related needs. Rule #1 in riding is "Safety first," but Rule #2 should be "Appropriateness in all things." So when your child goes to the barn for her lessons, it's critical that both rules be followed scrupulously.

The following list should be appropriate for most beginning riders. Always check with the riding instructor before you buy, however, as many lesson programs have specific attire requirements.

- ✪ A certified riding helmet
- ✪ Sturdy boots with a heel
- ✪ Stretchy riding pants that won't bunch or ride up
- ✪ A comfortable shirt that's appropriate to the weather

Clothing should fit fairly snugly and be comfortable. Many instructors discourage loose or baggy clothing as this can obscure what the rider is doing with her body. (Is she slouching in the saddle or is her jacket bulging around her? Is her knee positioned properly?)

Because riders, especially young ones, approach riding because of love for the horse, there's a tendency sometimes toward informality and comfort. This can translate to wearing sneakers and shorts, skipping the hard hat on a hot day, and perching bareback on a horse and popping a can of soda.

There are two sure ways to get hurt around horses: one is to rush or force them too quickly into doing what we

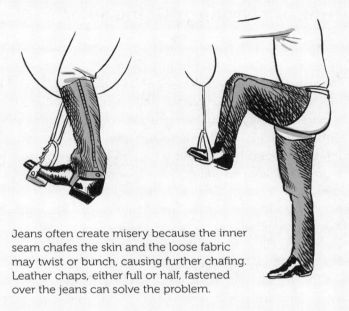

Jeans often create misery because the inner seam chafes the skin and the loose fabric may twist or bunch, causing further chafing. Leather chaps, either full or half, fastened over the jeans can solve the problem.

want; another is blatant carelessness. It is critical that your child understand the potential danger involved with being around an animal that is as fast and strong as a horse. Yes, she loves them. And yes, in horse books and movies, the horses are utterly reliable and intelligent and calm . . . But in real life, even the most reliable horse can have a bad day or can be startled.

Talk with your child and ensure she understands how important these rules are, since you may not always be there when she rides:

- ✪ Always wear a certified hard hat when mounted.
- ✪ Always wear good riding boots.
- ✪ Always respect the horse's power.
- ✪ Never rush or be careless.

Getting in a Group or Going Solo?

There are two basic types of lessons: group and private. Most beginning riders should start in private lessons, as this allows the instructor to focus solely on the child and allows the child to focus solely on riding, instead of finding her way around the arena in a potentially distracting group of horses and other riders. Once your child is proficient, though, group lessons are usually more economical, as the rates tend to be lower when the instructor is teaching several students at once.

Group lessons generally consist of three or four horse/rider combinations and typically run about one hour. All the riders in the group should be at the same competency or skill level. The horse your child rides in the lesson needs to behave appropriately in a group — even though they're herd animals, some equines do not like feeling crowded.

When the instructor determines that your child is ready to safely participate in a group lesson, there are many benefits to having her do so. Here are just a few:

- Group lessons provide your child with a great way to get to know other horse-crazy kids.
- Riding with other children is great fun and helps to encourage your child's efforts to make friends in the barn.
- Group lessons give students the opportunity to observe the instructor's directions to other students, which helps to develop your child's "eye" for correct riding practices.
- Group lessons help students learn to maneuver safely in an arena with others, which she will need to learn if she is interested in competing at some point.

Learning from the Ground Up

As herd animals, horses are fundamentally social beings, and although they make a variety of vocalizations, they do not rely significantly on sound to communicate with one another except over distances. Instead, they speak volumes through touch and through body posture. So for humans to effectively interact with horses, we have to use their own methods of communicating, in effect, to speak their language.

The first, most critical step in doing this is working with the horse from the ground, not in the saddle. One of the most crucial elements of ground handling is grooming, which involves more than the obvious purpose of cleaning the horse before putting on his saddle and bridle. Grooming lets the handler and the horse get to know each other through touch and up-close body language.

Correct grooming techniques gently communicate to the horse that humans have the right to handle him — brushing his body, lifting his feet, putting equipment on him — which establishes the handler as higher in stature or herd dominance. And because the handler, by effectively exerting his or her dominance, isn't hurting or frightening the horse, the horse realizes the handler is trustworthy and not to be feared.

For all the positive elements of effective ground handling, there are some potential negatives. A handler who uses a curry-comb roughly on a horse's tender skin, for example, communicates unkindness and indifference. A handler who flinches from a horse's snort or a tail flick communicates fear. A nervous handler usually creates nervousness in the horse, who may feel that there's something nearby to be frightened of so he should be on his toes and ready to spook. More serious issues arise when the horse interprets nervousness as a sign that the handler is not a suitable herd leader, and therefore, the horse becomes pushy, ignores reprimands or corrections, and perhaps even acts aggressively.

Do-It-Yourself Grooming and Tacking Up

Everything that ultimately happens in the saddle begins on the ground. Because it's very common at lesson barns for each horse to be ridden by many students, every successive student must establish and reinforce her relationship with the horse every time she works with that horse. It may seem that a lesson barn is providing great customer service when the staff prepares the horses before every lesson and students just show up and climb on; but actually this is an incredible disservice to both the student and the horse.

Barns that require students to handle their horses on the ground, and to groom them and tack them up, are not getting their horses cleaned up "for free" — they're teaching essential horsemanship skills and beginning the critical, and immensely rewarding, steps toward developing a positive and appropriate relationship between horse and rider, before the student ever climbs into the saddle. This kind of close interaction helps to build confidence in the student and provides her with terrific satisfaction and even joy, since part of the pleasure of riding is working with the horse at all stages.

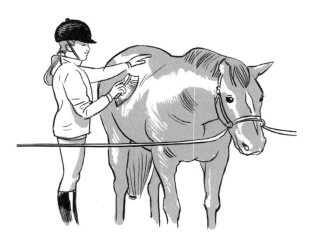

Your child's favorite time at the barn may be spent grooming — before a lesson to become acquainted with the horse and afterward to rub out the sweat marks and reward the horse for his work. At the end of it, she'll come out smelling like a horse — which, to a horse person, is way better than any rose.

Basic Barn Manners

Smoking is never, ever allowed in a horse barn or arena. This is because pretty much everything you'll find in these areas is highly flammable — hay, grain, feed chaff, not to mention wooden barns and fences — and also because horses generally do not react well to smoke. For all horse owners, the potential of a barn fire and resulting tragedy for the horses is among their greatest fears. Seeing someone smoking in the barn area will usually provoke an angry response.

> Everything that ultimately happens in the saddle begins on the ground. It's critical, therefore, that the relationship between horse and rider be established early and be reestablished every time the student goes to the barn.

Never run around horses, yell, toss or throw anything, or make any sudden movements. Don't open or close umbrellas, shake out blankets or jackets, and so on when horses are anywhere nearby.

Never tie a horse with the reins of the bridle. Use only a lead rope and halter to tie a horse, and only when a safety or quick-release tie is used.

Leave your dog at home. While some dog owners may think that letting Fido meet the horses would be a great idea, few barns allow it. Many dogs have a natural tendency to bark and lunge at the horses, to chase the barn cats, and to, well, act like a dog. None of this behavior is welcome at most barns, even those that have a dog or two of their own.

Safety First

If a horse becomes panicked — whether he's tied and struggling against the tie, or he's thrashing about in a stall, or he's gotten loose and is bolting around the barn aisle — absolutely get out of his way. Never try to step in and catch an out-of-control horse if you don't know what you're doing.

Etiquette in the Arena

Just as there are rules of the road for driving a car, so, too, are there rules for riding horses. Unlike the written rules for driving cars, however, most of the rules about riding are learned through experience and the examples set by those around us. For obvious reasons, it's important that all posted rules related to riding in an arena be followed explicitly.

Although some of the following descriptions may not apply to your beginning rider, it's important to know what is expected in any situation. These warnings are not intended to instill fear — if anything, mentally anticipating reactions to the environment helps to control fear because it puts the rider in a greater position of control and readiness.

- Unless your child's instructor directs otherwise, riders should mount prior to entering the arena (if there is a safe space for mounting, with sufficient head space) or mount in the center of the arena, completely out of the traffic flow.

- Ideally, all rider/horse combinations in the arena should be working on the same type of activities — jumping, for example, or flat work (that is, practicing the different gaits such as the walk, trot, and canter). Even more ideally, all rider/horse combinations in the arena should be very close in ability and skill level.

- When in the arena, slow-moving horses stay on the rail so that faster-moving horses can easily and safely pass them on the inside.

- It is a good rule of thumb for a rider to call out "passing" as she approaches a slower moving pair, although this doesn't always happen and can't be counted on. Therefore, prior to moving off the rail or picking up speed, it is an excellent practice to look over one's shoulder and ensure that it's safe to do so.

- When we drive cars in the United States, we move in opposite directions with our left shoulders on the inside. The same is true in riding, which is key to know when riding in a crowded arena.

- Riders must be constantly alert to other riders' actions, speed, and direction, as well as the mental attitude of the other horses — unlike cars, horses have their own opinions about the goings-on around them and may kick or strike out unexpectedly.
- Riders should keep two to three horse lengths between themselves and the closest rider. If someone is having difficulty controlling her horse, other riders should find a clear path to move safely around the unhappy horse, leaving a great deal of space, and then keep their distance.
- Horses should never be longed (worked on a line) in the arena when others are riding.
- In the event that another rider falls off her horse, everyone in the arena should immediately stop their horses and turn them to face the fallen rider.
- Whooping and hollering, kicking the horse's sides, flapping the reins, and generally acting like a Hollywood version of a cowboy is never allowed. Riding quietly and calmly, with respect for the horse and for others, is the proper etiquette.

Parental P's and Q's

As they do with every other pursuit their children engage in, parents want to provide support and encouragement and long to see their child do well. Sometimes, though, these wonderful intentions get the better of us and we act in a way we would never do otherwise.

Particularly because nonequestrian parents simply don't have enough knowledge or experience to know what's considered appropriate (or inappropriate) behavior, they may feel uncomfortable in a barn environment. Feeling comfortable is, of course, about more than just fitting in. Parents want to take an active role in their children's activities, to understand the learning process, and, in general, to participate and be engaged.

But how do you do this when you feel like a fish out of water? No worries — it really isn't difficult at all. You just need to know a few things about navigating your way around a barn.

Here are some ways you can assist your child in her learning experience, with tips on how to interact with the instructor, with the other parents, and the trainer's staff (running a horse business takes a lot of effort).

- If your child cannot make it to a lesson, notify the instructor at the earliest possible moment.
- Always show up on time and have your child ready to go — appropriately dressed, riding boots on, helmet in hand.
- If your child is young enough to need reminding, make sure she has gone to the bathroom before mounting the horse.
- Pay the invoices on time — riding facilities have constant expenses to cover because horses always need to eat, barn workers need to be paid, and farms always have ongoing projects.
- If you have questions for the instructor or an issue to discuss, save it for a time when she is not interacting with students and you have some privacy. You should always feel comfortable asking the instructor questions — just pick a good time to do so.
- Do not talk to your child during her lesson, whether you are pleased with her progress or annoyed at her behavior. If you think she is being whiny or disrespectful, wait until you are in the car to discuss it. Never reprimand your child in front of the instructor or other children.
- Unless everyone is being positive and encouraging, do not discuss riders' skills with other parents. Some riders will learn faster than others — this is natural. Young riders do not need to be reminded of their perceived errors or mistakes.
- Do not negatively discuss the instructor or the barn staff with other parents. If you have a concern, talk to the instructor directly or go to the barn owner or manager.

You're Still the Parent

One of the most important rules about any kind of lesson is to let the instructor teach. The only exception to this is if you feel that your child is being pushed unsafely beyond her skills (for example, you can clearly see that your child is unsteady at the walk, cannot keep her feet in the stirrups, keeps dropping the reins, and is struggling to remain mounted, yet the instructor is asking your child to jump). This is not the same as your child being asked to try the next step in a logical progression of skills (for example, your child can sit the walk confidently and securely, so the instructor asks your child to trot).

If your child is genuinely distressed about something, you should absolutely step in and remove your child from the lesson. The entire point of this is that it be *fun*. If your child is fearful or crying in a lesson, not only is it not fun, it's also potentially dangerous because some horses react to their rider's emotional state — a frightened or fearful rider may result in a frightened horse. If the instructor doesn't have your child dismount and leave the arena until she is calm, then you need to intervene.

Remember: You are the parent. You do not abdicate your rights or responsibilities when your child steps into the barn. You always have the right to intercede if you think a situation is potentially harmful.

TO WATCH OR NOT TO WATCH?

Even though every barn is different, parents tend to wait in one of two places while their child is in a lesson: in a viewing stand next to the arena (not all barns have seating areas, though) or in the comfort of their own car.

If you opt to remain by the arena to observe the lesson, be sure not to hang on or sit on the rail. It's distracting to the riders and horses as they come by and could actually cause a horse to spook. (And it causes undue stress on the fencing material itself!) Wherever you decide to wait, however, make sure that your child is happy with the choice; some children may be nervous to have a parent observing the lesson, whereas others might find it thrilling to have an audience. Just ask your child what she'd prefer.

If you do form the habit of watching the lessons, look for opportunities to encourage your child, as well as the other riders. You don't have to know the specifics of what each is doing or understand the nuances of riding any more than you need terrific detail to encourage kids in a soccer or baseball game. As you

Learning to ride is a joyous, challenging, tiring, and ultimately wondrous experience — noting each child's efforts along the way will mean the world to them.

watch the children mastering each skill, like proceeding from walking to trotting, from trotting to cantering, make a point of congratulating them (after the lesson is over). Just telling them they looked great or were sure working hard is enough.

Riding 101 — Why Are They Just Going Round in Circles?

For the nonequestrian, watching horses and their riders going endlessly around and around the arena can be not only perplexing but also about as exciting as watching paint dry. But with experience, you'll realize there is much to be seen with each circuit. There are nuances in the horse's movement — he's striding out more, he's maintaining a more constant speed, he's able to keep on a straight line (much more difficult than you'd think), he's going well into the corners, he's bending better in his circles, he's picking up his leads nicely, and much, much more. This kind of observation is very useful to the learning process and interesting to a viewer who can see the improvements or note the mistakes.

For the nonequestrian, however, it may be a bit of a struggle to find something interesting in the carousel-like trips around the arena, over and over and over . . . ! If you're planning to watch a lot of lessons and would like to know more about what's going on in the ring, it might help to begin with a discussion of what the instructor and rider are working on, what they're doing, and what they're trying to accomplish. So we'll begin by explaining the horse's gaits and how the instructor gauges the skills of horse and rider.

Riders must learn what the correct position feels like, train their muscles to be able to hold it, and then to automatically assume the correct position whenever in the saddle. The back should be straight with good upper body posture. The head should be erect with the chin level and eyes gazing in the direction of movement. There should be a straight line from the center of the rider's head through the shoulder, elbow, hip, and heel, and a straight line from the rider's elbow through the hands and reins to the horse's mouth. Heels must be down and toes up.

Working at the Walk

You'll be seeing a lot of this gait, especially at first. It may seem boring to go around the ring at the walk, yet the rider is learning quite a lot. Your child is thinking about all the issues mentioned below while keeping her balance, moving with the horse's motion, remembering how to hold the reins, trying not to tug on the horse's mouth, and myriad other details. As you watch, look at the quality of the walk and ask yourself these questions:

- Does the horse move in a balanced way, with a willing attitude, at a steady and measured speed?
- Does he keep a straight line along the rail or does he wander back and forth?
- Does he bend his body as he goes around the corners or does he keep it rigid?
- Does he stay at a calm walk or does he jig and dance with impatience to go faster?
- Is the horse "on the bit" (his head is perfectly vertical) or is he ahead of or behind the bit?
- And how about the rider? Is her seat "deep" or does she appear ill at ease and loose in the saddle?
- Are her hands gentle, yet keeping good contact with the bit — in other words, moving forward and back in harmony with the horse's natural head motion at the walk?
- Are her heels down and toes up?
- Is her lower leg jammed against the horse's side or are they properly straight and maintaining a very light contact?
- Does the rider slump in the saddle or maintain good posture?
- Does the horse/rider pair look in harmony or do they appear stiff or uncomfortable with each other?

A wonderful way to show your child you're enjoying her riding almost as much as she is is to videotape her. Play the video at home and have the whole family watch, and encourage your child to talk about what she's doing onscreen and why. Still photos can be used the same way.

Watch the Horse's Head

While the rider must achieve and maintain the proper position, the same is true of the horse. The rider's position is intended to help the horse carry her, and the horse's position helps him move in the most balanced way possible.

Incorrect: This horse is "ahead of the bit," meaning that his nose is stretched out too far and the reins are too loose (note his uncertain expression and ear set).

Correct: This horse is "on the bit," with his head perpendicular to the ground and good contact between his mouth and the rider's hands. The relaxed ears and facial expression indicate the horse is content and comfortable.

Incorrect: This horse is "behind the bit," meaning that his chin is too close to his chest because the reins are held too tight. His flattened ears and flared nostrils indicate his discomfort.

Talking the Talk

Grooming. Brushing and combing a horse's or pony's body, mane, and tail, as well as cleaning out the hooves.

Gait. The pace at which a horse moves forward. Most horses have four gaits — the walk, trot, canter, and gallop in English; the walk, jog, lope, and gallop in Western.

Collection. When a horse assumes a rounded, flexed, and balanced posture, which helps to increase his physical ability to comply with the rider's requests. A horse can be collected at all gaits.

Contact. The connection, through the reins and the bit, between the rider's hands and the horse's mouth, which should be firm but without strain or tension.

On the bit. The horse is accepting the bit and the rider's contact. This can be observed by the horse's head position, which should be vertical to the ground when viewed from the side. A horse who is "behind the bit" will have his chin closer to his chest; a horse "ahead of the bit" will have his nose ahead of his forehead.

On the rail. When the horse and rider are moving along in the arena, next to the fence or rail.

Transitioning to the Trot

The horse and rider must master the qualities described at the walk before trotting — speed does not make these skills easier to attain! The trot is a two-beat gait much like a human's jog, in which the diagonal legs (left front and right rear, right front and left rear) hit the ground at the same time. The most common trot is the "working trot" — a steady, brisk speed at which the majority of training is performed. There is also the western "jog," a slow but steady two-beat gait; the English "collected trot," a controlled, elevated trot for higher level work; and the upper-level dressage "extended trot," a lovely gait at which the horse's legs really stretch and reach.

Some horses' trots are naturally lovely and springy, which makes them easy to ride once the rider gets the hang of how it feels. Other horses (particularly ponies) are cursed with hard, jolting trots that make this gait difficult and uncomfortable for the rider. For this reason, as well as to save the horse's back from being pounded by the beginning rider's seat, riders "post." This is when the rider, moving in concert with the horse's stride, alternately rises slightly and sits back in the saddle (for this reason, a posting trot is also called "rising trot.")

The Difference Between Posting and Sitting Trot

Posting is done "on the diagonal," using the shoulder toward the outer side of the arena. So if the horse is circling clockwise, his left shoulder is the outside shoulder. The rider rises slightly out of the saddle when the left foreleg steps forward at the trot and sits back gently as the leg moves back — this is called posting on

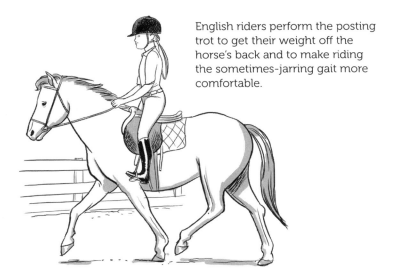

English riders perform the posting trot to get their weight off the horse's back and to make riding the sometimes-jarring gait more comfortable.

the left diagonal. If the right shoulder were closest to the outside of the arena, as is the case when circling counterclockwise, the rider would post on the right diagonal. It takes a lot of practice to post properly and to remember when (and how) to change diagonals.

Riders also must learn to ride the "sitting trot," which, just as it sounds, means that the rider remains seated in the saddle. This is actually harder to do well than posting, because it involves maintaining balance, proper leg position, proper seat position, and soft contact with the horse's mouth. It takes quite a bit of experience to develop the ability to remain elegantly seated and move *with* the horse's motions, instead of banging up and down *against* the horse's trot.

Controlling the Canter

After your child has mastered the basic skills at the walk and trot (which could take months), she will be ready to think about cantering. The canter is the gait between the trot and the much faster gallop (your child will not be doing this in lessons!). The canter is a three-beat gait and is intended to be collected (controlled) and pleasing to watch. It's moving at speed, but calmly. In contrast, the gallop is a four-beat gait, where you can hear each hoof striking the ground individually.

> Although the idea of riding at the canter can be a little intimidating because it seems fast, the canter is actually an easier gait to ride than the trot. This is because of the rocking motion of the horse's body while cantering.

At both the canter and the gallop, the horse "leads" with one foreleg or the other, meaning that either the left or the right foreleg reaches farther forward as the horse takes a stride. The horse leads with the leg that is to the inside of the ring, allowing him to balance better and bear his weight more correctly in the turns. In other words, when the horse is "on the left lead," the left foreleg reaches farther ahead than the right; on the right lead, the right foreleg reaches farther ahead. If the horse is circling the arena counterclockwise, he should be on a left lead; if he's circling clockwise, it should be the right lead.

When your child is riding at the canter, learn to figure out which lead she is on and whether her hands and heels stay down — the natural tendency for beginning riders is to tighten their body and draw up as the horse's speed increases, so the heels come up and the hands rise. Remaining deep in the seat, keeping tension out of the arms and hands, and keeping the lower legs in the proper position rather than swinging with the horse's rocking motion are the major tasks your child will work on as she learns to canter. And none of this is easy or intuitive! It takes a long while to get all of this right and to do it all consistently.

One of the biggest milestones your child will achieve at some point in her lessons is successfully riding the canter. The gait is smooth and rocking, and the speed is exhilarating. The first time she canters is cause for celebration!

Ongoing Assessment

After your child has been taking lessons for a while, how do you determine the continued safety of the lesson programs and appropriateness of what's taught? In many ways, you can follow your own instincts. What do you see when you observe lessons? If the instructor starts teaching your child to jump, for example, and you can see that your child can barely steer and stop the horse, you need to put a halt to things.

As you watch your child's lessons and talk to your child afterward, ask yourself the following questions:

- Does your child like the instructor and enjoy being around her?
- How well does the instructor interact with the students? Does she know them all by name?
- Do the students feel free to ask questions and discuss their concerns with the instructor? Does the instructor take time to listen and respond to the students?
- Does the instructor provide positive feedback?
- Does the instructor offer constructive criticism without scolding or harping?
- Is the instructor patient with *your* questions? Is your involvement and participation encouraged and welcomed?
- Can the instructor discuss details about your child's progression off-the-cuff and in a detailed, thorough manner?

In some ways, learning to ride a horse is not unlike learning to drive a car. The instructor doesn't just hand over the car keys and tell the student to have fun. The beginning driver has to learn about safety features, about the rules of the road, how to use the brakes to stop smoothly, how wide to take a right or a left turn . . . just starting the car can take a while to master!

It's no different with riding, except that the horse is a living, breathing creature with a mind of his own. It is essential, therefore, that riders learn how to handle the horse on the ground (catching, leading, tying, grooming, tacking up), as well as in the saddle (how to steer, how to stop, how to stay in the saddle, to develop a balanced seat and soft hands, and so on) before ever pursuing more advanced activities that require a solid foundation. Going straight to jumping, for example, would be like taking a 15- or 16-year-old driving student and putting him on the Autobahn at 120 mph.

FROM A HORSE-CRAZY KID

When I was about two, my mom and grandmother took me out to Sandy Lake Park where they had pony rides. After my first ride was over I did not want to get off my pony. I started crying and throwing a fit because this first experience of riding was about to be over. The man who was running the pony ride allowed me to continue riding for free until I almost fell asleep on the pony that afternoon. From then on I was hooked.

To me, horses have always meant beauty, freedom, and an art of communication between an animal and a human. I have always been content to watch horses all day. When I was little, my riding buddies and I pretended to be horses and would personally jump over anything we could stack up. We would set up courses for our dogs to become the latest and greatest "horse" in our backyard.

The kindness of horses' hearts captivates me. It is amazing how a person's kind actions and words can erase a horse's memory of wrongdoing and prior experiences with cruelty. How the horse, if treated right, holds no grudges.

— *Ciearra*, age 12

Is My Child Ready to Move Up?

In the equestrian world, riders must earn the right to study and perform at higher levels by first mastering the foundation skills at the lower levels. Otherwise, serious injury to both the rider and the horse is all too likely. The topics that follow should be considered as a guide for assessing your child's readiness to move to higher training levels.

Assessing Your Child's Interest

Before determining if your child is ready to move on to a higher level of instruction, it's important to be sure she is still enthusiastic about riding. Ask yourself the following questions, and of course, ask your child what she wants to do.

- Does your child still enjoy going to lessons and being around horses?
- Does she drag her feet and allow relatively minor details to prevent her from going to the barn or interacting with the horses?
- Is your child usually eager to be at the barn, even in inclement weather or when another activity conflicts with it?
- Is she reluctant to leave the barn when it's time?
- Does your child actively seek out the horses when arriving at the barn?
- Does she have a favorite who is often the recipient of special pats and treats?
- When handling horses, is your child relaxed and confident?

Another aspect of assessing readiness is to observe her progress. When watching your child on horseback, ask yourself if she can adequately control the horse. Look for the following signs:

At the halt. Does the horse stand quietly or is he jigging around and tossing his head?

At the walk. Does the horse maintain a steady walk, go in the direction your child tells him to, turn and stop as your child cues him? Do your child's feet remain in the stirrups? Do your child's feet consistently maintain the proper heels down/toes up position? Is she sitting quietly in the saddle, relaxed and comfortable? Can your child maintain the proper length of reins (a straight line from the hands to the bit, neither taut nor loose)?

At the trot. Can your child maintain her seat in the saddle?

At the canter. Is your child comfortable and enjoying the speed and the experience? Can your child maintain her balance at the greater speed? If the horse were to give a happy little buck, would your child be able to handle it (both physically and mentally)? Can your child maintain control of the horse at the canter and maneuver safely and confidently around other riders/horses or obstacles?

If your child can do all of these things consistently, comfortably, and is still enjoying the experience, then and only then should jumping a very small jump be considered. And, by the way, jumping is not something anyone ever *has* to learn to do — it is just one of many disciplines riders can learn.

Parent and Instructor Roles

The decision to move a student on to higher training levels is a tough one — even for skilled instructors. This is because it takes a combination of mental and physical readiness: a professional instructor can easily determine the physical skills but no one can read another person's mind, so mental readiness can be challenging to evaluate.

This is when the instructor–student relationship becomes particularly critical and when the instructor's experience, skill, and knowledge truly are put to the test. Some students, for example, don't have enough confidence in their increasing skills to believe they are ready to move on to bigger challenges. They may require extra coaching, extra encouragement, and (sometimes) being pushed a bit to take that next step. A skilled instructor, therefore, has to figure out how to help the student to develop self-confidence and to appropriately recognize (and believe in) her own abilities.

Another challenge for instructors can be students who have a burning desire to move on to higher training levels, but who simply don't (yet) possess the physical skills to accommodate that desire. The instructor in this case must carefully channel those ambitions into building the foundation skills, yet keep the student from becoming bored while doing so. Even more important, she must prevent that student from putting herself into a potentially dangerous situation that exceeds her ability to handle.

Just as critically, how do parents, lacking the instructor's skills and knowledge and experience, know when their child is ready to move to higher training levels? How do you know when your child is being pushed too fast or held back too much? How can you tell if the training level is safe and appropriate for your child? And how can you tell if you are the one either holding your child back or pushing her too hard?

It starts with observation and ongoing involvement — regularly observing your child's riding lessons and seeing for yourself your child's progress and engagement, her interaction with the instructor, how the instructor encourages your child and how your child responds. Listen to the instructor's evaluation, even if there are aspects of it you don't want to hear. Then listen to your own parental instincts. No one knows your child as well as you do, after all.

4

Children
with
Special
Needs

Horseback riding can be a tremendous equalizer. Historically, this factor has applied mainly to gender, as this is one of the few sports in which men and women compete equally (although some would argue that women have a slight edge on men due primarily to a lower center of gravity and lighter body mass). But far more important than gender, riding offers equal opportunities for individuals with special needs.

A wonderful example is James Taylor, who in 2007 traveled to China to compete in the Special Olympics World Games, where he won a silver medal in dressage, a bronze medal in equitation, and took fourth place in trail. James has also been honored with Equest's Levi Strauss Award.

Another rider, Stacey Johnson, has ridden at Equest for more than 15 years and has traveled to Washington, D.C., as an ambassador for the Special Olympics Athlete Leadership Program. Stacey, along with other Special Olympics athletes from across the United States, met with senators and representatives to help pass a bill appropriating funding for Special Olympics.

Finding Financial Aid

Many health care companies, upon the recommendation of a treating physician, will provide benefits coverage for hippotherapy. As well, some therapeutic riding centers offer scholarship aid or a sliding fee scale to assist families with the expense of therapy sessions. Check with your health care company and your physician to determine the level of coverage available to you or your child.

How Horses Help People

Sitting on the back of a gentle, well-trained therapy horse means liberation from a wheelchair or crutches and freedom from physical limitations. Horseback riding can ease the body's movement and soothe discomfort; it promotes balance and helps to train neurological pathways to function in a way that allows the body to move in a correct manner. At its most basic (and perhaps most meaningful), riding provides the pure joy of connecting with another living creature — one who doesn't judge, who isn't critical, who treats each and every person equally and equably.

A surprisingly wide list of conditions have been studied at length and proven to benefit from hippotherapy:

- Amputation
- Attention Deficit Disorder
- Autism
- Brain Injuries
- Cardiovascular Accident/Stroke
- Cerebral Palsy
- Deafness
- Depression
- Down Syndrome
- Emotional Disabilities
- Learning Disabilities
- Mental Retardation
- Multiple Sclerosis
- Muscular Dystrophy
- Spina Bifida
- Spinal Cord Injury
- Visual Impairment

Why Use Horses in Therapy?

Other than being fun, how does riding a horse help individuals with such a broad range of disabilities and conditions? A major component of the answer lies in the way horses move — at the walk, for example, the horse's movement mimics the way human hips move when we walk. This close similarity helps train the brain and related muscles of a body that struggles to walk.

Riding also aids physical coordination, builds muscle strength, and improves balance. The reaching and stretching of the muscles during riding is beneficial for its therapeutic value.

Unlike more traditional methods of physical therapy, which typically occur in hospital settings or offices, therapeutic riding takes place in a natural environment with fresh air, open spaces, and all the pleasures of being around horses and barns. And then there are the horses themselves. Besides being nonjudgmental about their riders, think about the sensory aspect — they have silky manes and tails, their breath is warm and hay-scented, their whiskers tickle, they make delightful sounds when they snort or whicker, their coats are sleek and smooth, the rhythm of their steps is soothing . . . the feel and sound and smell of horses add a range and depth of sensory stimulation you just can't get in a hospital or office.

Because people tend to focus more on things they enjoy, therapy becomes an event to be welcomed and looked forward to, making it all the more effective.

In a typical therapeutic riding session you'll see a coordinated team of individuals surrounding the horse and rider — a therapist, a horse handler, and one or two walkers supporting the rider.

A major factor in the success of therapeutic riding is the boost it gives to the rider's self-confidence. Disabled riders are mastering a task that the majority of nondisabled people cannot do — they are riding a horse, controlling a large animal, and doing so in a skillful way. And while most riders who participate in therapeutic programs begin with a focus on therapy, a respectable number go on to high-level competition, even at the international level. The Special Olympics and the World Games, to name two such events, have taken disabled riders around the world to compete in some of the finest equestrian venues in existence. How's that for a confidence boost!

Finding a Therapeutic Riding Center

To qualify as a therapeutic riding center, the facility must have not only gentle horses and people who want to help but also support from knowledgeable staff who are thoroughly familiar with the challenges special needs riders face and how best to assist them. To find a center with the appropriate level of skill, knowledge, facilities, and horses, look for a facility accredited by NARHA, Inc. (formerly the North American Riding for the Handicapped Association).

This 40-year-old association has established standards for safety, education, communication, and research; with more than 5,500 members and more than 730 programs in the United States, NARHA is recognized for its dedication to promoting excellence in therapeutic riding programs. It offers three levels of certification for riding instructors: registered, advanced, and master. Canada has a similar organization, called the Canadian Therapeutic Riding Association (CanTRA). Founded in 1980, CanTRA has approximately 100 member centers across Canada that provide high-quality therapeutic, recreation, life skills, and sport programs.

Talking the Talk

Several terms are used to describe the therapeutic use of horses for individuals with special needs. The main terms are:

Hippotherapy (from the Greek *hippos,* meaning "horse"). Sometimes referred to as "equine facilitated therapy," this type of therapy is facilitated by a professional physical therapist in conjunction with a professional horse handler, often with the assistance of knowledgeable volunteers who walk alongside. The goal is to improve neurological functioning in cognition, body movement, organization, and attention levels. Sessions are private, with the therapist utterly focused on a single patient in order to continually assess and modify therapy based on his or her responses.

Therapeutic Riding. Sessions, usually for a group, are led by a professional riding instructor in conjunction with volunteers, including a physical, speech, or behavioral therapist who may be involved as a consultant. The goal is to provide social, educational, and athletic opportunities through riding lessons adapted for individuals with disabilities.

Whatever the name, the positive effects of riding on individuals with a wide variety of disabilities is significant, particularly in terms of increased muscle tone, improvement of postural control, psychological benefits, and balance.

Specialized Tack and Equipment

Correctly and safely matching a rider with the proper equipment requires the expert knowledge of a certified therapist. Consider the variety of tack and equipment needed to work with a horse and then add the specialized needs of disabled riders. Each individual rider has particular requirements in order to be safe in the saddle, and a qualified facility will have all the necessary equipment. Safety stirrups, bitless bridles, reins that can accommodate hands with limited movement and strength, adaptive equipment such as bolsters and wedges, nylon fastening tape for students who cannot use saddles, and more — there are ways to make it possible for nearly anyone to ride!

In addition to standard mounting blocks, specialized mounting ramps that can accommodate wheelchairs are critical to ensuring that all riders can safely mount their assigned horses. And the horses must be trained to calmly accept all the efforts that go into helping a disabled rider climb aboard.

Therapy Horses

Like nearly every horse facility, most therapeutic riding centers operate on a tight budget. Therapy horses are often donated, generally after having served as a show horse or lesson horse for most of his life. But not just any horse can become a therapy horse. The key criteria is that the horse be gentle and kind,

Riders with special needs come in all shapes, sizes, and ages. But they share a love of horses and the dedication and drive to put that love into action.

patient and steadfast, with the disposition to stand quietly at all times and remain unflappable regardless of what goes on around him. Therapy horses know to move out carefully and are mindful of the rider's balance.

Therapeutic riding centers take great care in evaluating and selecting horses for their programs. And they take superb care of these horses, recognizing them for the rare treasures that they are.

FROM A HORSE-CRAZY KID

I have always loved horses, especially since I was nine. My mom has, too, but she didn't have any as a kid. Now, though, she and my dad both ride for fun.

At first, I didn't want to ride; I just liked to groom and bathe horses. When I started lessons, though, the horses were pretty big and I could only reach as high as the belly, which made grooming harder.

I have two former ranch horses now. They're both gelding Quarter Horses. I ride them Western pleasure and would like to do trail, since they're both very responsive. My horses' names are Ike and 88.

Ike and I have a total connection and we know what we're each thinking. I know Ike loves me because we have a really strong bond.

Just after I first began riding, I decided I wanted to quit — the Texas summer heat is really bad and I have a problem with heat. But I had a few friends at the barn who talked me into staying. And now, I want to ride always. Even when Ike is bucking, I'm having fun. Riding is so comfortable, it's a nice getaway. Some people sing — I ride.

— *Caroline*, age 14

5

On with
the Show:
Classes
and
Clothing

The first question on your mind is probably this: "Is it necessary for my child to show horses?" The answer is a qualified "no." Becoming a competent, even accomplished, rider does not depend on riding competitively. Nonetheless, going to horse shows can be a tremendously valuable experience for a young rider because the excitement of preparing for a horse show is balanced by the very real patience and hard work that are necessary for that preparation.

Showing horses is one of those rare experiences when your child will be learning important life lessons without even knowing it. One lesson is that hard work usually *does* pay off in the show ring, in which case, your child has the opportunity to learn how to win well. If someone else worked harder preparing or just has better luck that particular day, your child has the opportunity to learn how to lose well. These are both wonderful lessons to learn.

To a child, taking "her" horse out in public, riding in competition, and testing her own skills against other riders with similar levels of experience is exciting and enjoyable. Learning to handle herself and her horse in a variety of situations develops problem-solving and organizational skills, showcases the benefits of hard and focused effort, demonstrates how to set goals and plan to achieve them, teaches how to take responsibility for another living creature, and reinforces the importance of following through on commitments — these and other lessons will stand your child in good stead throughout her life.

Types of Competition

Horse shows exist for all levels of riders, from the rawest novice to the international competitor, and they offer a bewildering variety of classes in every conceivable discipline. It is beyond the scope of this book to cover them all, but we've included descriptions of the most common types of shows.

Most beginning riders who are working hard to improve their skills love the opportunity to dress up and participate in "schooling shows." These consist of a series of classes made up of groups of horses and riders. In each class, the horse and rider enter the arena one-by-one. Once the entire group is in the arena, the gate is closed and judging begins. Each rider performs as the caller instructs; for example, "trot your horses, please, the class should be at the posting trot." The riders are allowed two or three strides to urge their horses into a posting trot. The judge then gauges

As in most sports, riding offers much to be enjoyed and much to be learned — how great when both happen concurrently!

Talking the Talk

Equitation/horsemanship. A type of competition riding that judges the rider's skills and proper positioning, ability to handle the horse, quietness in the saddle, and so on.

Gymkhana. Gymkhanas consist of games on horseback that test the rider's skills and the horse's compliance and training.

Pleasure class. A type of competition riding that judges the horse's manners, movement, responsiveness, and way of going; in short, the degree to which the horse appears to be a pleasure to ride.

each horse/rider combination before having the caller give the next instruction; for example, "canter, please, the class should be at the canter."

Schooling shows do not focus on one particular discipline, such as dressage or jumping; rather, they are focused on the schooling or training levels of the competitors. Schooling shows also exist for inexperienced horses.

What's a Gymkhana?

Gymkhanas and play days are other wonderful venues for riders who are perfecting their foundation skills. These gatherings, which have the feeling of a fun, relaxed horse show, consist of games on horseback that test the rider's skills and the horse's compliance and training. The spoon ride, for example, requires riders to carry a spoon in one hand (or even between their teeth!) with an egg precariously balanced in the bowl. The competitors ride across the arena to see who can cross the finish line first without dropping an egg. The giggling alone makes this all but impossible.

Gymkhanas are games on horseback, all of which are terrific fun (and often funny, as when the horses try to participate in bobbing for apples), but they also help to reinforce riding skills like a deep seat, good balance, mounting without assistance, and so on.

Another fun game is bobbing for apples, which starts with a group of riders sitting on their horses at one end of the arena. At a signal, they race to the other end, dismount, hold on to their horses' reins, then dunk their heads into a barrel of apples floating in water. Once they get an apple in their teeth, they pull it out of the water, climb back on their horses, and race to the opposite end of the arena still holding onto the apple. Again, the giggling makes getting hold of an apple impossible, and the horses often want to participate since they can smell the lovely apples.

Bareback dollar or ride-a-buck is another class you might see. Competitors ride with a dollar bill placed between their thigh and the horse's bare back while complying with the announcer's directions to walk, trot, and canter around the arena, just as they would in any other class. As each rider loses her dollar bill, however, she has to move to the center of the arena and stand quietly. The last person whose dollar bill is still in place wins the class — and all the other competitors' dollars, too!

Types of Classes

The kind of classes that your child might participate in will depend on the discipline that she is pursuing. If she rides at a show barn with a particular area of expertise, she will be guided through the various stages of, say, dressage or hunter/jumpers. Other barns leave the decision of which shows to attend and which classes to sign up for to the students.

Some types of classes overlap both English and Western riding, others are specific to one style or the other. Both styles of riding have two basic divisions: pleasure classes, and equitation (English) or horsemanship (Western) classes. Pleasure classes primarily judge the horse's manners, movement, responsiveness, and way of going; in short, the degree to which the horse appears to be a pleasure to ride. Equitation and horsemanship classes, however, primarily judge the rider's skills and proper positioning, ability to handle the horse, quietness in the saddle, and so on. Horses that compete in pleasure and equitation classes must be solid, reliable, and comfortable. They are responsive to their rider and do not easily become alarmed.

In addition to these basic classes, each style of riding offers a number of different options — something of interest for every rider. Classes are divided into levels from novice to expert, and, in many cases, competitors earn points in order to move up to a higher level of competition. Following is a brief discussion of the most common disciplines in English and Western riding.

The Main English Disciplines

Dressage is popular with many English riders, as it can be pursued at any level of ability. This sport judges a horse's calmness, responsiveness, and grace, as well as the rider's skills, in a complicated test of riding patterns (for example, circles, figure eights, straight and diagonal lines across the arena) at varying gaits and ways of movement (extended or collected — see box), which the rider must memorize. With its focus on the relationship between

It's all over but the announcement — riders and their horses stand center ring as they await the judge's decision.

horse and rider, dressage is a lifelong discipline that offers continual opportunity for improving horsemanship skills and refining the training of any horse.

Hunter and jumper classes test the ability of both horse and rider over a course of fences. The jump heights range from low (two feet) to quite high (over six feet), depending on the skill and experience of the competitors. In hunter classes, the emphasis is on steadiness, calmness, and a clean round (not hitting the fences or knocking down rails). Hunters (the term also describes the type of horse, though not a specific breed) must have impeccable manners: kicking, for example, is inexcusable because of the danger it creates in the hunt field. A hunter-type horse is calm and willing, not easily spooked or alarmed, and has a long stride and terrific stamina.

In a jumper class, the focus is on speed — clearing the fences in the least amount of time. The horses, while expected to mind their manners, are not judged on their behavior, just their ability to finish the course quickly and with no rails down or jumps refused. Jumper-type horses share the hunter's natural talent for and love of jumping, but they tend to be much faster and "hotter," meaning they are more excitable and spirited.

Collection and Extension

In many disciplines the horse is expected to change its way of moving while staying within the same gait. This is particularly true in dressage classes, where the test includes demonstrating this change at three gaits (walk, trot, and canter). In a collected gait, the horse is said to be moving "in a frame," meaning that his head is vertical to his chest, his neck is nicely rounded, and his stride is measured and precise. When moving at an extended gait, the horse carries his head somewhat in front of the vertical and reaches his legs well forward, taking long and energetic strides.

Cross-country riding takes jumping out of the show ring and into the country, back to its roots in foxhunting. Riders gallop along a course of solid, fixed fences (heights and complexity of the jumps depend on the level of competition) and various natural obstacles such as water and hills.

Three-phase eventing (or just **eventing**) is a true test of horsemanship, comprising cross-country, stadium jumping, and dressage. To compete successfully, both horse and rider must be sufficiently skilled and conditioned to complete a long and demanding cross-country course, to memorize a pattern of jumps in an arena and clear the obstacles with speed and precision, and to perform a dressage test with grace. Eventing horses must be fast and agile for jumping; have terrific stamina, courage, and strength for cross-country; and be calm, flexible, and responsive for dressage.

Hunt seat and hunter under saddle are classes that judge horse and rider on the flat (no jumping). In this style of riding, the rider sits deep in the saddle, following specific traditions of clothing and horse tack that come from fox hunting. Horses that do well in these classes are well-mannered and calm.

Saddleseat is a very particular type of competition that was developed in the United States to demonstrate the animated movement of high-stepping breeds such as the Saddlebred and the Tennessee Walker, whose natural movement is usually encouraged with the addition of heavy, weighted shoes. This is not a discipline for beginners. The horses who are most competitive in the show ring are spirited and fast, and their training is highly specialized (and controversial, as it may involve "soring," a process of creating chemical burns on the horse's lower legs to encourage him to pick up his feet, and other harsh methods).

The saddles (called "slicks") are flat, small, and constructed of very smooth leather. Given the horses' "hot" disposition (which is both bred for and "encouraged" through handling and training), the challenge of maintaining one's balance while riding a very animated, high-stepping gait is beyond a beginner's capability and absolutely beyond that of a child.

The Main Western Disciplines

Reining is similar to dressage in that horse and rider perform a memorized pattern of movements at different gaits. The concept is that the movements are those used by cowboys working cattle. Reining movements include circles, spins, and stops, as well as the breathtaking sliding stop in which the horse gallops at top speed across the length of the arena, then plants his back feet and slides to a complete halt. Most of the movements are performed at the lope, which is a slower, more relaxed version of the canter.

Reining competitions are great fun to watch, even for non-equestrians, because of the grace, speed, and responsiveness of these horses. Plus, the competitors are not just going round and round — you can really see how well one horse reins as compared with another, which allows everyone to enjoy the skill and grace on display.

Barrel racing, a popular rodeo event, is a timed race at top speed around a cloverleaf pattern of barrels. The trick is to race flat-out on the straightaway and slow just enough to make the tight turns as close as possible to each barrel without knocking them down. Riders who love speed thrive in barrel racing and the same is true of their horses.

Cutting pits horse and rider against a single calf or cow who must be separated from a small herd of cattle. The pair must keep the animal away from the herd while she dodges, darts, feints, and attempts to sprint past them in order to return to her fellows. Cutting is exciting to watch and a real thrill to ride. It's not the easiest discipline for the beginner, however, as the best cutting horses are "cow smart" and lock on to the separated animal with total focus — which means the horse is dodging, darting, feinting, and sprinting faster than the cow. The rider needs to have an excellent seat and terrific balance in order to stay with a hardworking cutting horse!

Ranch Horse competition tests the Western horse and rider on all skills necessary to succeed on a ranch. Incorporating trail, cutting, roping, reining, team penning, barrel racing, and even pole-bending, Ranch Horse competition thoroughly tests the skills and abilities of both the horse and the rider in each of its many classes. These competitions are great fun to watch, and competitors with all levels of experience have opportunities to compete, since most Ranch Horse shows include youth and amateur divisions.

Trail is a class in which the horse and rider must maneuver through an obstacle course and complete a series of activities such as opening and closing a gate, putting on and taking off a rain slicker, crossing a mock bridge, dismounting and remounting, and carrying a big garbage bag (usually filled with newspaper) and putting it in a trash can.

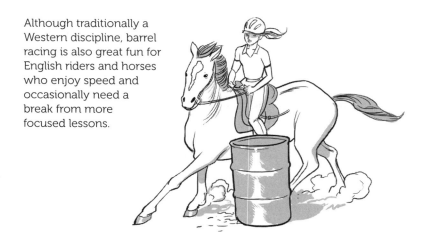

Although traditionally a Western discipline, barrel racing is also great fun for English riders and horses who enjoy speed and occasionally need a break from more focused lessons.

Some Other Types of Classes

Lead line is a class for the youngest riders (on experienced, often geriatric horses), who are led by an experienced adult handler. The child is judged on poise, balance, and proper position. The horse or pony is judged on cleanliness, calmness, and appropriate (and safe) tack. The child is led around the arena in both directions at the walk only and may choose to hold the reins loosely or to simply hold on to the saddle's horn (if Western) or strap (if in a lead line–style or English saddle). Children who attempt to steer their horse or pony (with the leader for backup) will usually place higher than children who just sit on the horse's back passively. These classes are taken seriously by judges and spectators alike — as they are by the child competitors — and all of the children receive a ribbon and the enthusiastic congratulations of everyone involved.

Walk/trot classes are for young or inexperienced riders or horses; only the walk and trot are performed.

Halter is typically a class in which the horse is shown "in hand," meaning that the handler leads rather than rides. The horse's conformation is judged, as well as his manners and how well he moves at the walk (and sometimes at the trot, with the handler running beside him).

Halter showmanship is very similar to halter, except that the horse's grooming, his actual halter and lead, the handler's skills, and the handler's attire are judged more closely.

Costume class means, literally, that the rider and horse are wearing a costume. In these classes, only the imagination (and safety) limit choices. Some classes are "anything goes," while others have a theme, such as Arabian or medieval.

Not all showing takes place in the saddle; halter classes test handling skills from the ground.

What to Wear: A Guide to Show Attire

If your child is interested in showing or if your lesson barn requires them, proper show clothes will be essential. The expense of dressing your budding equestrian, however, doesn't have to be prohibitive as long as you go with a list in mind and know exactly what it is your child really needs — and you don't buy any more than that, even though temptation (and sometimes anxiety) might lead you to purchase much more.

Always check with your child's instructor before making any purchases. Some disciplines have quite specific requirements for show attire. For example, competing in dressage calls for somewhat different clothing than hunter/jumper classes. In some instances, distinct but unwritten preferences can affect how the rider is judged, and as with all fashion, the trends change. The following descriptions are for the typical formal outfit required for English and Western riding; ask your instructor for guidance in selecting clothing for your child's particular discipline.

Proper English Show Attire

As described in chapter 3, helmets and boots are the fundamentals of any English riding outfit. Your child will already have a schooling helmet for lessons, and with a black velvet cover, it might well serve for competition, even at a more formal show. In some cases, however, a traditional black velvet hard hat is required. These hats have a trimmer design than a schooling helmet, but the construction is solid, with a rigid visor and a sturdy strap to hold the hat on securely — again, always check for ASTM/SEI certification.

As for boots, you will eventally have to invest in a pair of dress (tall) boots. Paddock or jodhpur boots are not acceptable in competition, except for the youngest competitors, who wear them with garter straps below the knee to prevent the legs from riding up. Tall boots come to just below the bend behind the rider's knee and for competition purposes must be solid black.

Buy a Boot Jack!

An extremely useful tool for wearing riding boots of any style, but particularly tall boots, is the boot jack — a wonderful invention that allows a rider to remove boots without assistance. (This device is especially appreciated by the parents of these riders.) The suction created between a tall boot and a sweaty foot is such that the wearer can easily be pulled across the floor as a well-meaning parent pulls and tugs strenuously in an effort to remove the boots, which are often dusty at best, muddy at worst, and always covered with a variety of "barn germs." Do you really want to wrap your hands around them?

Only in training or day-to-day informal riding is any color other than black acceptable.

Dress boot styles differ in the narrowness through the calf area and the outside height — for example, dressage riders often prefer a slimmer boot through the calf with a taller outside design referred to as "Spanish style," which gives the visual effect of a longer leg. Tall boots with laces at the ankle are called "field boots" and are seen in the foxhunting field but not usually in the show ring. "Hunt boots" have a brown band or cuff at the top, with the remainder of the boot in black, and are traditionally worn by adult male riders with significant hunt field experience.

English Riding Pants

Two styles of riding pants are available to English riders: jodhpurs and breeches. The jodhpur (pronounced "JOD-per") traditionally fits somewhat loosely; some styles even flair at the thigh. The design slims at the knee and is snug through the lower leg, often ending in a cuff at the ankle. For jodhpurs worn outside the boot, elastic stirrup straps that attach to buttons on the inside of the cuff and go around the bottom of the boot's instep are extremely useful for keeping the jodhpur from slipping up while riding.

Jodhpurs are worn mostly by young riders before they graduate through experience and age to breeches. Jodhpurs are usually buff-colored (appropriate for daily riding as well as for the show ring) but are also available in subtle colors and even in patterns, such as plaids and houndstooth, for riders who wish to express their personality when riding in lessons or for fun.

Breeches are slim and stretchy pants that fit closely to the rider's body from waist to ankle. When worn with a tall riding boot, the breech leg fits inside the boot. When worn with paddock or jodhpur boots, the breech is always paired with either a half-chap or full-chap for comfort and to protect the lower leg from potential pinching by the stirrup leather, which is painful and can leave a nasty bruise.

Traditionally, the breech is worn by older and more experienced riders, as it clearly defines the leg's position. Breeches are acceptable for young riders for daily use, however, because they are comfortable, are often made of lighter-weight and stretchier fabric than jodhpurs, and allow terrific range of motion.

In the show ring, breeches are usually a buff color, although dressage riders wear white ones (hence the term "dressage whites"). Some of the newer breech fabrics come in absolutely wild colors and patterns, providing terrific fun and personal expression. Prices range from quite economical to insanely expensive.

Jodhpurs with paddock boots and gaiters

Breeches with tall boots

English riding pants of all types have some form of additional coverage on the inside of the calf and knee (called the knee patch), which not only protects this tender skin from being pinched by the stirrup leathers but also provides extra grip on the saddle. The material used in both jodhpurs and breeches helps create a more secure seat in traditional, smooth-leather English saddles, which can sometimes be a little slick.

English Shirts

English shirts are traditionally long-sleeved and collarless; have a slim, tailored fit; and are made of crisp, white cotton that holds a crease beautifully, although some of the more fashion-forward disciplines (like jumping) may allow a subdued color that complements the riding jacket and the horse's coat color. Sleeveless versions are acceptable in informal shows and for training.

English shirts can have one of two neck styles: a collar that wraps around (somewhat like a priest's collar) and usually fastens with a bit of Velcro in back or a traditional stock tie, which is a long length of matching material, two to three inches wide, that is tied around the neck like a cravat. Both styles are finished

Wearing Gloves

While not necessary for daily use, in horse shows, dressage competition, and formal exhibitions, the riders will normally wear gloves. Black gloves are most common and appropriate at all skill levels, with a benefit to less experienced riders that the color somewhat disguises faults such as wobbling hands or imperfect position.

White gloves do just the opposite, of course; riders who wear this color glove have achieved such a high skill level that it is appropriate (and expected) for them to display their perfect hand position. For this reason, riders must traditionally *earn* the right to wear white gloves.

with a small, simple gold or silver pin at the throat. In addition to looking elegant and crisp, the stock tie can still serve its original safety purpose — it can be used to wrap a horse's wounded leg or to splint a rider's arm in the hunt field.

English Jackets

The riding jacket or coat is imperative for horse shows, formal exhibitions, and dressage competition, and each style of riding has its own style of coat, although the differences can seem very slight to the inexperienced eye. They come down to nuances such as the number of buttons, the type of vent in the back, the style of waist, the color, the collar style, and so on. Dressing appropriately in the horse show world is absolutely critical, as it displays an awareness of one's own position in it (based on years of experience and skill), knowledge of etiquette and appropriateness, and respect for equestrian traditions.

Whatever the discipline, a nicely fitted riding jacket shows the rider's lines (arm placement, posture, balance) clearly enough for judges and instructors to gauge skill and overall positioning. The impression created by the rider's attire and the horse's tack should be elegant, scrupulously clean, and pleasing to the eye. To this end, when competing in English disciplines that allow jacket colors other than black, riders are very conscious of selecting shades that go well with their horse's coat color — brown, for example, makes a pale gray horse look yellowish, so a dark navy or black jacket would be better.

Proper Western Show Attire

The clothes traditionally worn by Western riders have a long and hardworking history, and they have evolved over centuries of wear and tear by individuals whose lives were spent in the saddle and working cattle. The clothes reflect the grueling lives these individuals led, as well as something of the spirit of the American cowboy. Consequently, Western clothes must first be functional and durable, able to stand up to a hard, honest day's work in the saddle. But that doesn't mean the clothes have to be boring — some of the most beautiful, handmade leather- and silver-work can be found in Western clothes, saddles, and bridles. And some Western pleasure outfits are electrifying in their colors and designs.

So whether for a day riding cattle in Montana, riding broncs at a Texas rodeo, or competing at the prestigious Quarter Horse Congress, the clothes must help their wearer get the job done and look good while they're doing it. This means that when we talk about Western clothes, it's important to acknowledge their function and uses, as well as their style.

The Issue with Western Hats

Cowboy hats are typically made of tightly woven straw or well-made fur felt, capable of holding water for thirsty horses to drink from (or to be dumped over the owner's overheated head after a long day in the saddle). Cowboys use their hats to fan balky embers into a suitable campfire or to signal one another over distances. They also provide shade from the sun's fierce glare and shelter from torrential downpours. While the traditional colors for cowboy hats are subtle — tan, white, cream, brown, or black — today's hats, especially styles for women, are offered in every shade imaginable.

Although the traditional cowboy hat has no safety features that will protect the rider's head in the event of a fall, newer hats (especially those made for young or inexperienced riders) actually do contain a solid shell that offers protection. You will find that protective headgear is not required in most Western

> Be sure your child's attire fits the discipline and her own skill level. And, just as in any other area of fashion, what's "in" can and does change within the riding world, although often quite subtly. It is essential, therefore, to have the experienced guidance of an instructor or a helpful tack store salesperson.

competition, and might even be subtly discouraged; yet, the risk of falling off a horse exists no matter what the discipline, and it is your right as a parent to insist that your child ride safely. More and more Western riders, even tough rodeo riders, are beginning to wear helmets. Many also don protective vests, which should be considered for any equine sport that is performed at speed or over fences.

This young rider and her pony are in Western tack and attire, ready for a Western pleasure show class. The long-sleeved button-down shirt, comfortable jeans, a nice leather belt, and a good pair of Western boots (note the heel) came right out of her closet.

Cowboy Boots

Cowboy boots provide the same safety benefits as English boots and have the same components — a good heel, a solid sole for side-to-side protection, and a good toebox to protect the foot from a careless hoof. Unlike English boots, however, which can be tall (dress boots) or short (paddock boots), Western boots come to about mid-calf on the wearer. They can have a rounded toe, a boxy toe, or an amazingly pointed toe — the type depends on the kind of riding and the rider's preference.

Traditionally, Western boots do not have laces of any kind and come in subdued neutrals of tan or brown. The finest cowboy boots can fetch astronomical prices, being handmade of exotic skins such as ostrich, anaconda, or elephant and having intricate designs and vibrant colors. These types of boots are generally worn to special events rather than the barn.

Western Riding Pants

Western-style pants are made of strong fabric, usually canvas or denim, that resists damage caused by riding through underbrush, yet still holds a crease and looks nice. Blue jeans work perfectly well, can be purchased affordably, and when constructed with a bit of stretch, are extremely comfortable to ride in. Jeans, worn with or without chaps, are acceptable in virtually all types of Western competition.

Western Shirts

Think of cowboys and you probably think of the Western "yoke" design on cowboy shirts and jackets. Western-style riding shirts are usually made of lightweight cotton and fit trimly without restricting movement. Traditionally, shirts are light-colored to help deflect the sun's intensity. Subtle plaids are common, especially for men and boys, although women and girls also wear them, especially in competition divisions like ranch/working horse, reining, or roping. Western shirts are sometimes paired with a vest, which is usually made of leather and often incorporates beautiful hand-tooled designs and embellishments.

Paying Attention to the Details

The kerchief typically worn by cowboys performs the same function as the English rider's stock tie, with the added benefit that it can be dipped in water and used to wipe a sweaty face, tied around an overheated neck to offer some relief on a hot day, or used to cover the mouth and nose during a dust storm. In the show ring, they offer another chance for the rider to display a dash of color and pizzazz.

No Western outfit is complete without a well-made leather belt and beautiful buckle. The best of these are handmade and contain silver, turquoise, and coral; the most highly prized are often made by Navajo artists and fetch incredibly high prices. Perhaps the most respected buckles, however, are those won through competition at shows or rodeos, many of which are made with fine crystals and semiprecious stones. Some of these buckles are enormous, as is the pride with which their owners wear them. It is considered disrespectful to buy such a buckle and wear it without having earned it.

The full-length chap is also integral to the Western outfit, although not all disciplines use them. Clearly, when working cattle in heavy undergrowth, chaps are essential to protecting the cowboy's legs from harm. Chaps are also useful when working around cattle on foot, as a stray hoof or horn tip could otherwise slice right through a pair of pants, even durable denim or canvas. In the show ring, chaps can offer an additional touch of glamour, as in Western pleasure classes, or can pay homage to the traditions of the cowboy, as in cutting competition, although the added protection can be useful when working cattle in the tight quarters of an arena.

Glamour in the Show Ring

Western clothing offers fun opportunities for self-expression and flat-out glamour in the show ring, though as with English, it's critical to check with the instructor before going to the tack shop for the first time to buy riding clothes. Women's show clothing can come in every vibrant color of the rainbow, studded with glitter and sequins, in every pattern imaginable. The shirts, called "slinkies," can be slim and tight fitting and are often paired with handmade vests covered in complex detail and designs. The ensemble often includes gorgeous full chaps with intricate designs of their own, heavily encrusted leather belts, and big, shiny buckles.

Western show clothes can be purely functional (but always immaculate and pressed to a knife-edge crease) and worn by boys or girls. But girls have the added fun of wearing wild and colorful riding clothes in any pattern.

The horses are also dazzling in their show tack — Western saddles and bridles are often beautifully hand-tooled and decorated with sterling silver and intricately woven leather and can be paired with saddle pads that match their riders' clothing. Under the spotlight of an evening exhibition, these rider/horse combinations bedazzle the eye with their finery.

A Word about Spurs

It's worth spending a minute on spurs and their uses in riding, although keep in mind that an inexperienced rider has no business wearing spurs, period. Wearing spurs without the ability to use them effectively is unsafe for the rider, as well as potentially cruel to the horse, and is considered utterly inappropriate by knowledgeable horse people. Riders who have achieved a certain level of skill and developed a quiet, still lower leg could consider wearing them; they are regarded as something of a badge of honor by knowledgeable riders, who place the well-being of the horse above their own vanity.

When used by a talented, skilled, and experienced rider, spurs are a tool — an extension of the lower leg — and are used to touch lightly or to apply gentle pressure, never to gouge or poke or dig. Spurs can be invaluable at higher levels of horsemanship, providing an additional cue to the horse and what is required of him.

English spurs are different from their Western counterparts familiar to most of us from the movies. English spurs are usually silver; they are quite small and elegant-looking, and have a slim strap that goes over the top of the foot's arch and buckles under the instep. There are many styles — some end in a molded, round knob and others in a small disk or rowel that rotates when in contact with the horse's side.

Perhaps even more than English spurs, Western spurs should never be worn by inexperienced riders. With their longer shanks and larger rowels, some Western spurs, if used carelessly, have the potential to cause serious damage to the horse's sides.

As with English riders, Western riders earn their spurs and to wear them without having earned them is to be considered fake or a "dude." And, just like in English riding, Western riders use spurs as an extension of their legs but with a greater focus on soliciting speed. With so many varieties of Western spurs available, the style chosen by the experienced rider tells others something about that individual's chosen discipline and riding preferences.

CRAZY ABOUT HORSES

I've always been horse crazy, but have been riding for three years. I know exactly when I began riding — October 2005.

My parents lease a Pony of the Americas mare for me. Her name is Ruby and she's 20 years old. I like that she can jump and that she's older, so she doesn't have too much *oomph* for me. She's a small horse, but she's very powerful. Ruby loves to go to horse shows and gets worked up, which doesn't help, because then we're both nervous. She's also a princess and definitely has boundaries. But she's not mean, she just likes to have things her way.

I will always want horses in my life, living with me. It would be really nice to look out my window and see horses. But I want older horses, 15 to 25 years old. This is the perfect age for me.

— *Brooke,* age 10

I would definitely describe my daughter as being horse crazy. She rides every chance she gets, her bedroom is decorated with nothing but horses, and on every calendar, she's written the words "maybe I can ride today."

Brooke has gained self-confidence from riding and being around horses, which I think will help her throughout her life — having the ability to handle a horse with confidence will help her to follow her own will, to set her own limits. Being around horses is the most wonderful thing Brooke has experienced.

— *Melanie,* Brooke's mom

What's All This Going to Cost?

Parents often wonder if riding gear, especially formal show attire, has to be bought brand new. The answer is absolutely not. Children outgrow riding clothing as quickly as their regular clothing, and parents everywhere share this frustration. But they can also share hand-me-downs! Your barn is the first place to look for used clothing, and your instructor is a good resource.

Check with your local tack stores to see if they have any gently worn boots and clothes for sale — most tack stores will have a consignment area where these items are displayed. Most online retailers offer items on sale (see Resources for Parents for some suggestions). Local riding clubs are an excellent source for good-quality clothes and equipment. You can purchase the entire outfit your child needs at a fraction of the amount you'd spend for new clothes. And when your child outgrows them, there's a great market for you to sell them to other parents.

The one exception is that you should never buy a used riding helmet, even one that is certified. This is a piece of equipment you should never skimp on or purchase used. You won't know if a used helmet has already taken a number of hits, thus compressing the protective material inside it and making it less effective at protecting your child's head. You also want to be sure it conforms closely to the shape of your child's head, which a used one may no longer be able to do.

6

Behind the Scenes at a Show

You and your child have been working toward and imagining all the things that will take place in the ring in front of the judges and spectators. Excitement has been building, and now it's Showtime! Well, almost. . . . Before she rides elegantly into the ring, there are many tasks to be done to put your child at ease, to keep her horse happy, and to be sure everything is in order for every event she plans to enter.

Working with the instructor, you can have several important roles. Before the show, you're the scheduler and driver; during the show, you're the ground crew, unflagging cheerleader, diplomat (with the other parents), fashion assistant, and photographer/videographer. But your job doesn't end when the show's over — then you become the historian, since one of the great pleasures for riders is rehashing, in terrific detail, everything that occurred on the momentous day.

Talking the Talk

Premium. This guide to scheduled classes is distributed before a show.

Green as grass. A class for first-time competitors, this description can apply to either rider or horse.

Vintage. Designating a class for riders who are 45 years of age or older, this term is used as an adjective, as in "Vintage English Pleasure."

On deck. The competitor waiting to go next in the ring is said to be "on deck" and is typically expected to wait in a particular spot.

Before the Classes Begin

From the minute your group arrives at the show grounds, the instructor will be extraordinarily busy, even if she has brought along senior students or assistants to help. Making sure the horses are settled and safe is of extreme importance, so seeing to the horses is the instructor's first focus. Some shows offer stabling for the horses, so before unloading the horses, the instructor will find the stalls assigned to them and inspect each stall to make sure it's safe and sturdy, and she will probably set up the stall by spreading shavings for bedding, hanging water buckets full of fresh water, and putting in some hay before unloading the horses and stabling them.

This way, the horse comes off his familiar trailer and goes straight into a comfortable stall. If the horse is thirsty from a long trailer ride, there's fresh water ready. And if the horse is nervous about being in a new place, having hay to eat will often distract him and help him settle down.

If the horses will not be stabled on-site during the horse show, then they will be showing "out of the trailer." This means the participants' horse trailers are parked together, with enough space to safely tie horses on either side of each trailer, and to walk or lead a horse between the parked trailers. The riders will likely have to dress and change clothes in the trailer's tack room (if it has one) or in the back of the trailer — often necessitating a cleanup job first, because horses always seem to pass manure the moment they're loaded onto a trailer.

Finding the Facilities

Some show grounds have dressing rooms or large bathrooms, which makes dressing in the trailer unnecessary. This still requires good organizational skills to plan enough time to collect the show clothes, go to the dressing area, change clothes, return the original clothes to a car or the trailer, and be ready for a class. Chances are good that your child will have several wardrobe

Transporting the Horse

If your child is riding a lesson horse from the barn (or you lease or board a horse at the lesson barn), chances are good that the instructor will trailer the horse to the show. It's quite common for many riders from the same barn, learning from the same instructor, to attend horse shows together. It's great fun and a wonderful way for your child to learn to show — under the guidance of the instructor and in the company of friends.

It is common practice for the instructor to charge a trailering fee for each horse taken to a show, but if the instructor doesn't mention this, it is fine for you to broach the subject. Practices vary from instructor to instructor, so make sure you know what is expected. Generally, the trailering expense is based on the distance from the barn to the show and back; often, instructors use IRS mileage reimbursement guidelines to determine an appropriate per-mile charge.

changes during the course of a show, so parents can help out by collecting the already worn clothes, keeping track of what is needed for the next class, and knowing where every outfit is.

Showing out of a trailer can also be a chore when you or your child needs to go to the bathroom, since this will probably entail having to walk some distance to find the facilities. Occasionally, there will be portable toilets available, which is handy, but generally there's no way to wash your hands afterward since there's typically no sink. Bringing along sanitizing wipes or lotion is a fantastic idea for this reason.

Understanding the Instructor's Job

In addition to seeing to the horses and managing their students, instructors handle the tons of paperwork associated with horse shows, from Coggins test results for each horse (if they were not sent in with the mailed entry forms and fees), to ensuring each rider's entries were received and properly recorded, to obtaining the class schedule and barn assignments, to picking up the "back numbers" assigned to each rider (a number printed on paper that is pinned to the rider's back so the judge and announcer can identify each rider/horse combination), to figuring out where to park the trailer. Getting everything in order can be challenging — especially if the instructor has a number of riders and horses at the show.

On top of everything, each horse must be prepared for his class. This entails not just grooming but also braiding the mane (if it's required for the show or if the instructor is so inclined), tacking up, and then riding the horse in the warm-up arena before putting your child in the saddle. The instructor will probably have your child ride in the warm-up arena so she can warm up, too, and work out any perfectly understandable nerves. A warm-up ride helps the horse and rider to reacquaint themselves with each other in a new environment, to mentally prepare for entering the show ring, and to remind themselves that they can *do* this!

Slogging through the Paperwork

You probably won't have much involvement in the show paperwork itself, other than to write the check to cover the entry fees and the instructor's expenses. But it's helpful to have an idea of the process of signing up for a horse show. There will always be a release statement or liability form that requires a parent or legal guardian signature.

There will be at least one page that lists the classes in order of how they will be held at the show, including a class number. For example:

In-Hand (Halter) Classes	Performance Classes
1. Handler Ages 6–8	4. Lead line Pleasure
2. Handler Ages 9–11	(English or Western)
3. Handler Ages 12–14	5. Walk-Trot English

It is important on show day to know the number of each class in which your child will compete, since the announcer will frequently just call the class number when calling competitors to be ready (on deck) to enter the arena.

Fees are generally determined by class, with amounts starting at $5 to $10 and going up, depending on the show's ranking, the experience level of competitors, and the venue (a highly rated equestrian center will generally cost more than a small county fair).

Reading the Premium

Every show, even the smallest, puts out a "premium" or guide to the classes offered. This is distributed before the show so that riders can determine which classes to sign up for and can plan their day according to the schedule of events. All competitors look forward to receiving the premium and spending lots of focused time studying, planning, strategizing, and anticipating the upcoming show. Reviewing the premium with your child is a great opportunity to spend quality time together and to share in her passion.

How to Enjoy a Horse Show

As a parent, your primary job at a horse show is to be an uncon-
ditional fan, to carry any extra clothing or equipment, to provide
a bottle of water on a hot day and a quick sandwich at lunchtime,
to help pull up tight breeches over sweaty skin, and to make
sure your child's back number is securely on and that her hair
is neatly secured underneath her riding helmet. It's helpful to
think of yourself more as a partner and less as a parent, because
"partner" connotes a job to do and shared responsibilities.

Once your child is in the ring, here are some guidelines for
being a good horse show spectator:

- Some show grounds have stands or bleachers; if not, you may
  bring folding chairs to sit on much as you would to watch
  a soccer game. Just position yourself well out of the way of
  horses and riders coming and going from classes.
- At most shows, it is considered rude to stand along the arena
  fence where you might block other spectators' views.
- Never sit on or put your feet up on the arena rails or fencing.
  It's considered disrespectful, may damage the facilities, and
  could startle the horses and riders in the arena.
- It's fine to skip the concession stand offerings and bring a
  cooler with snacks and cold drinks, but do not bring alco-
  holic beverages.
- Do not listen to a radio or music without headphones.
- Do not bring your dog. Dogs have no place at a horse show.

Horses Will Spook at the Strangest Things

While a horse show in many ways resembles any other sporting event, there is one factor that is very different: the horses themselves. Many of them are seasoned competitors who are not fazed by the many sights, sounds, and smells of the show grounds, but others are still learning how to cope in unfamiliar surroundings. Horses experience the world quite differently from humans, and even the best trained may react in a panic to items that seem completely innocuous to us. For example, tents and awnings flapping in the breeze can set a whole arena full of horses into a tailspin. Here are a few things to be aware of to minimize the possibility of a major spook or worse, a runaway:

- ✪ A jacket being put on or an umbrella being opened or closed near the rails
- ✪ Crackling chip bags, fizzing soda cans, and other unexpected noises
- ✪ A paper bag, napkin, or other trash blowing in the breeze
- ✪ Camera flashes
- ✪ Spectators talking loudly or gesticulating enthusiastically (keep an eye on younger siblings, who might be bored and restless)
- ✪ Standing or moving suddenly, especially when you're close to the rail
- ✪ Clapping
- ✪ Cigarette or cigar smoke
- ✪ A ringing cell phone
- ✪ Crying babies

And sometimes we just don't know what made a particular horse spook, because it didn't even register with us but certainly did with the horse!

Don't Forget the Hairnets!

The first few times you accompany your child to a show, you may be astonished at the amount of planning that takes place beforehand. Your child's instructor may handle much of the paperwork and most of the details of transporting the horses and kids, but you should plan to be available to help pack and check over lists. Aside from the obvious items like show clothes, helmet, and boots, the following items should be part of any standard show kit:

- Lip balm, sunscreen, and antiseptic wipes or lotion
- Bottled water, easy-to-eat snacks, a chocolate bar or two for quick energy, and something special that your child considers a real treat
- A camera with full batteries and plenty of memory for show photos
- A hairbrush, hair spray, at least two extra hairnets (if your child has longer hair), several hair ties or rubber bands, and a couple of bobby pins
- Several safety pins
- A rag for wiping off dusty boots just prior to entering the arena
- A box of tissues

Proper Parental Etiquette

Once your child is mounted and ready to go, your role is to step back and let the instructor take over. This is what athletes in other sports refer to as "game time" or "putting on their game." The instructor will be giving last-minute advice and observations, as well as a pep talk. Interruptions would be unwelcome and often, frankly, counterproductive. Instead, observe and listen, hold anything that needs to be held (gloves, a crop, a riding jacket, a bottle of water), and be ready to offer a jaunty thumbs-up should your child look your way . . . your quiet support will be greatly appreciated by both the instructor and your child.

Your child will most likely be focused on soothing the butterflies that invariably take up residence in even the most experienced competitor's stomach, calming the slight shakiness in the hands, and giving herself an internal pep talk. ("We can do this; we've been doing this forever in practice and now we're going to do it in this show.") Even loving and well-intentioned efforts to soothe nerves will distract from this internal effort — and learning how to calm and focus herself will be of tremendous benefit throughout your child's life. This skill is another of those life lessons that riding helps teach.

Once you've handed over whatever you're carrying and your child's jacket and gloves are on, with the back number neatly safety-pinned on, you can often tag along with the instructor and stand beside the arena together. Be sensitive of the instructor's frame of mind, however — some instructors are content to talk with you and tell you what they see in the arena, which can provide you with a wonderful horse show education; but other instructors are so focused on what's happening in the arena that carrying on a conversation is difficult. Think of your child's instructor as a coach observing a game of soccer or football and you'll better understand her feelings during a horse show.

Just as in football or soccer or softball or basketball, the riding instructor is a coach for both your child and the horse. This means that he or she has two athletes to prepare, to encourage, and to motivate.

This may seem obvious, but during the class, do not say anything negative about any of the other horses and riders in the arena. Without any doubt, the people around you also have someone in that arena and would overhear anything and everything you said. You would never want to hear someone speaking critically of your child and neither does anyone else. Being a horse show parent requires just as much good sportsmanship as is required of competitors!

Winning, Losing, and Other Life Lessons

When the class is complete and the competitors are all lined up in the center of the arena, awaiting the judges' decision to be announced, your child's heart will be pounding, her hands will be cold, as hope and expectation and anxiety and dread war equally. Many competitors are frantically trying to remember their back number because they can't see it. Others will be agonizing over their mistakes — perceived and real — and wondering if the judge saw their horse break stride or take up the wrong lead or spook on the turn . . . !

Listen to the announcer at all times. While clapping as a rider enters or leaves the ring is generally acceptable, if the announcer asks the audience not to clap for a particular pair, there's a good reason. Pay attention to what's going on in the arena. If the audience is clapping and a horse is beginning to spook, stop clapping and encourage those around you to stop as well.

This is the time to keep your eyes on your child and, if she meets your gaze, to give a big smile and a cheery thumbs-up. The sight of a supportive parent on the rail, smiling and silently applauding, does wonders, whatever the outcome.

The big moment arrives when the announcer calls the judges' rankings: first, second, third. In classes with very young riders, everybody usually gets a ribbon. Otherwise, somebody is going to win and everybody else is going to "not win," though as many as five or six riders may receive ribbons. There's a lot riding on parent etiquette in this situation — no pun intended.

Your child (and you!) must be prepared for all outcomes; how you behave will instruct your child on how to behave. If your child wins, you're entitled to clap and even hug the instructor. But don't go overboard — the other riders' families will be standing all around you.

It's proper etiquette for the riders to remain in the arena as all of the ribbon placements are called, so the audience is expected to remain at the rail or in their seats and applaud for each rider. Many shows allow the winning rider to take a "victory gallop" around the arena as the other competitors exit the gate; others do not, particularly those with a mix of young and inexperienced riders.

In either case, your child will be exiting at the gate; once all of the ribbon placements have been announced, it's fine to go to the gate and meet your child. Just stay clear of other riders who will be coming and going. The instructor will have your child dismount in a safe area and will then begin preparing for the next class, which may or may not have your child in it.

Following Up after a Class

Once a class is over, the instructor must leap ahead mentally to what needs to be done for the next class — which rider, which horse, which tack, which number, how much time — so do not expect to carry on a conversation at this point. When the show is over, there will be more time to talk, although the instructor will be thoroughly exhausted by then and probably just want to load the horses in the trailer and go back to the barn. Although sometimes, when things have gone exceptionally well, there can be an energized enthusiasm that makes everyone want to talk over every little detail right then while it's fresh.

The main thing is to be sensitive to the instructor's receptiveness to questions and conversation. In most cases, a warm "thank you" and an offer to help in whatever way you're able (carrying tack to the trailer, collecting grooming supplies, helping to pack up) will be appreciated, and you should probably wait for any conversation about specific classes until the next time you see the instructor at the barn. The exception to this would be if you have a grave concern or an urgent issue that you need to address in a timely manner. This would include a safety issue or a fairly serious transgression of sportsmanship, not a question of "I can't believe that judge didn't pin my child and what are you going to do about it?"

CRAZY ABOUT HORSES

I have loved horses since I was young. I am obsessed with horses! Almost everything I do involves them: drawing, writing, reading, watching videos, and taking pictures. I lease a horse at my barn and take lessons every week. I would love to some day own a tall gray Thoroughbred. Riding is the only thing I can do any day at any time. If I'm in a bad mood or having a bad day, I can go to the barn and forget about everything. I want to own a barn full of horses with my best friend. We plan on teaching, riding, and showing.

— *Julia,* age 14

Riding has become a wonderful way for us to stay connected and involved in our daughter's life. I strongly encourage parents to let their children follow their dreams when it comes to horses. When Julia began riding, she was very meek and quiet. Riding has given her a sense of self-confidence and a greater level of assertiveness, responsibility, and independence.

— *Brenda,* Julia's mom

In the Ribbons

Placement at horse shows is almost always announced in order, first place to the last place for which they're giving ribbons. Each show is a bit different in terms of how many places are awarded ribbons. Some give only first through fourth place, while others go all the way to tenth place. Here is a primer to explain placement and the color representing each:

- First: brilliant blue*
- Second: red*
- Third: yellow
- Fourth: white
- Fifth: pink
- Sixth: green
- Seventh: purple
- Eighth: brown
- Ninth: gray
- Tenth: pale blue

*In Canada, these colors are reversed.

At many shows, the highest scoring riders at the end of the day receive further recognition with the following ribbons:

- Champion: blue, red, and yellow ribbon; often with a large rosette, sometimes designed to wrap around the horse's neck
- Reserve Champion: red, yellow, and white ribbon, designed the same way as the Champion ribbon

7

Buying a Horse for Your Child (You Don't Have To!)

Chances are, your child has, at some point, asked wistfully for a pony or horse. Maybe it's a frequent request you've been hearing for years, or maybe your child has recently fallen in love with one of the lesson horses at the barn where she rides.

For someone who loves horses, there is simply nothing like the pure joy of having one of your very own. To care for a pony or horse and be its only rider is an especially heady thought for a child who daydreams about having a nonjudgmental confidante with kind brown eyes and a velvety muzzle, from whom a soft puff of hay-scented breath says more than all the words in the world. This imaginary cohort is always ready and happy to share a jog around the arena and to provide a warm and furry shoulder to cry on when needed.

Talking the Talk

Prospect. A horse that may be suitable for a certain discipline but doesn't yet have the necessary training.

Sound. Healthy, without injury or illness; used to describe both a horse's legs and his wind (breathing capacity).

Grade horse. A horse without registration papers; often of no particular breed or a cross of two breeds.

Cribbing. When a horse gulps air while biting down on a fence rail or stall door; considered a vice.

Vices. Undesirable behaviors exhibited by horses; can include cribbing, pawing, kicking at walls, and chewing wood surfaces.

The love affair your child has with horses in general, or one in particular, probably doesn't depend on a particular equine activity. Just being in the presence of horses brings its own sheer pleasure. Barns and stables are soothing places — the lovely, sweet hay aroma; the sun-dappled light streaming through open windows; the sight of a sleeping barn cat lying contentedly in a tolerant horse's feeder. And the horses themselves are such beautiful animals. The measured way they graze across a green pasture; the rhythmic crunch as they chew; the casual swish of a tail after a tickling fly; a soft *whicker*, deep in the chest — the sounds and sights and smells of horses create an inner calm.

So of course your horse-crazy child longs for a pony or horse to call her own! But there are many ways to give your child the deep joy of connecting with a particular, special horse or pony without having to take on the financial responsibility and unique needs of a very large animal.

Leasing a Horse

One option is to simply ask the instructor if your child can ride the same beloved school horse or pony in every lesson. This may or may not be possible, as each child in the barn will have a favorite and they often overlap. Also, some instructors feel that students learn more if they ride a variety of horses. If it is possible, however, your child might derive terrific satisfaction from the situation while continuing to build her skills.

If at some point you do find yourself tempted by the idea of horse ownership, consider first the option of leasing. Just as you can lease a car, you can lease a horse; in fact it is a quite common arrangement. And as with a car, leasing can be a lot more economical than a full-out purchase, especially with the added option of sharing a lease with another rider.

For any lease to be workable, you need to make sure that all of the details are sorted out in advance and are stated in a contract, which you and the lessor (the horse's owner) sign and date. In a shared lease, the expectations for and obligations of all three parties must be clearly spelled out and agreed to. The horse owner is typically responsible for drawing up the contract, but you might be able to ask the barn manager or your child's instructor for some guidelines. There are sample leases available on the Internet, but they vary widely in quality.

The Advantages of Leasing

As you begin to look into a more permanent relationship with a horse, consider your child's long-term interest. If her involvement with horses is still somewhat at the experimental stage, then leasing a horse and keeping him at the owner's barn or your lesson barn is the ideal way to explore eventual horse ownership. People offer their horses for lease for a variety of reasons, including lack of time to ride, ill health, going on sabbatical leave, and so on. Many barns also offer partial leases on their lesson horses.

A major advantage of a lease is that it is not permanent. Of course, if you buy a horse you can always sell him should your child outgrow him or become skilled enough to warrant a more advanced mount. With a lease, however, you can avoid that situation entirely.

Trudging to the barn in poor weather conditions to feed a horse or clean out a stall can tarnish all but the most deeply passionate individual's interest in horses. Even if you board your horse and don't have the daily tasks of caring for him, buying a horse and taking on his upkeep is a tremendous responsibility. By making a more formal arrangement in regard to a particular horse while continuing to interact with experienced horse people, you and your child will learn just how much commitment horses require — physical, emotional, and financial.

Signing a Full Lease

Each lease will have its own specifics and nuances, but there are two basic types of leases: partial and full. A partial or shared lease entails sharing access to the horse with another individual. A full lease provides you with the sole right to use the horse, just as if you owned him but without full responsibility for the horse's care, since you're likely to share vet, board, and farrier expenses with the actual owner.

If you're interested in a full lease on a horse, what will your responsibilities be? Here are some questions you should ask before signing any agreement.

What will be my share of the vet bills? Aside from unanticipated illnesses, horses need routine vaccinations, regular deworming medication, and annual veterinary exams.

What is my responsibility if the horse becomes seriously ill or is injured? Critical care costs can climb into the thousands very quickly.

What will be my share of the farrier bills? Most horses wear shoes and must have their hooves trimmed and shoes reset every six weeks, on average. New shoes may be required every other visit. Find out what the annual cost of shoeing is for this particular horse.

Will I be expected to pay half the cost of upkeep? The expense of feeding and housing a horse can fluctuate significantly. The cost of grain and hay is affected by gas prices and weather conditions. Boarding fees might be inclusive but some barns charge extra for blanketing, giving supplements or medications, and catching and holding your horse for the vet or farrier if you are unable to do so. Find out what the arrangements are where the leased horse lives.

Are there any limitations on the horse's activities? Will your child be able to take this horse to shows or out on the trail? When your child is ready for the next step in learning to ride (jumping or going on trail rides or showing or working cattle), will the horse's owner permit this? Does the horse have the experience, disposition, and physical abilities for this next step?

What if the owner decides to sell the horse while the lease is in effect? What if the horse dies or has to be euthanized? Your contract should specify your and the owner's legal responsibilities (and liabilities) to ensure fairness and adequate protection for all parties — as well as for the horse's well-being.

Whose Tack Do We Use?

If you lease a horse, the owner will most likely already own tack and grooming equipment for the horse and will prefer that you use them rather than buy your own. This is especially true with regard to tack, because the owner will have fitted the horse with a bridle, saddle, bit, and girth; if a lessee buys new tack (most likely a saddle that may fit the child better), it may not properly fit the horse.

This is important because poorly fitting tack can irritate a horse and lead to behavioral issues; a pinching saddle, overly tight girth, or inappropriate bit can create all sorts of problems. It's helpful to have your child's instructor involved in this process to ensure that the owner's tack fits the horse and is appropriate to his training level and disposition. Just because the owner has used a particular saddle and bridle on the horse doesn't necessarily mean it fits properly or that it's appropriate for your child.

Sharing a Leased Horse

If you're considering a shared or partial lease, the details discussed earlier become even more complex because another rider (either another child at the barn or the owner) would have access to the same horse. And while a co-lease significantly reduces your financial responsibilities, for such a situation to succeed it's even more critical that the details be worked out clearly and in sufficient depth, well before any issues arise. As with a full lease, shared leases should be formalized with a contract and signed by all parties — the lessor (owner) and everyone who will be leasing the horse.

Here are some questions that are specific to a shared lease:

- What days of the week will your child have the right to ride the horse?
- Are there specified times when the horse is available (or regularly not available) to be ridden?
- What about weekend use?
- What if one rider misses her scheduled day due to illness or vacation and needs to make it up?
- Is it acceptable for the horse to be ridden by both riders in a single day?
- If the students sharing the lease want to go to the same show, how will they share the horse equitably? (Especially if both children want to ride in the same class — a very real possibility if they are riding at the same level in the same lesson barn.)
- If this is a lesson horse, what will its lesson schedule be?
- Will your child have exclusive rights to the horse or will the horse remain in the lesson program? If so, will your child be given preferential access to the horse during her lessons?
- Will children who are not on the lease also be allowed to ride this horse?

As for upkeep and health expenses, be sure to spell out how the bills will be shared. What happens if the horse becomes ill and the vet bill is climbing? Suppose you and the owner are willing to split the costs three ways, but the other lessee wants a cap on what they'll spend. Who covers the difference? What if the horse is injured while the other lessee is riding him? Does that increase their financial responsibility and lessen yours? What if the other lessee no longer wants to ride — will you be expected to cover the difference in the horse's upkeep? Who will find another person for that half of the lease?

These issues illustrate why it is critical to address every possible detail up front, have them written into the contract, and get everyone involved to sign and date it. The best approach is to work out these details when everyone is calm and able to address the activity with a clear mind and no emotions. Never wait until there's a squabble over who gets to ride the cherished horse in an upcoming show or, much worse, who's going to pay for emergency colic surgery as the vet administers anesthesia. High emotions often result in bad decisions, not to mention lingering unpleasantness. So work out the details right from the start, when everyone is even-tempered and the exercise is intellectual, not emotional.

Making the Commitment: Buying a Horse

Leasing a horse is a wonderful way to ensure that your child is genuinely dedicated to the time, work, and commitment of owning a horse. Since the lease is such a great thing, why (and when) would you consider buying a horse? There can be several compelling reasons; for instance, if the horse your child has been leasing is being offered for sale and your child can't bear the thought of parting with him. Some leases include an option to buy the horse at the conclusion of the lease period.

Sometimes the owner decides that his or her life no longer has room for a horse in it and feels comfortable that you and your child would provide a good home. Just as a lease is a tentative first step toward horse ownership, it can (for a horse owner) be a tentative first step toward giving up a horse. Leasing a horse before buying him is a great way to know exactly what you are getting into.

You may also decide to make the commitment to horse ownership if your child has truly shown the dedication and grit to own a horse, has been riding for several years, and has been improving her skills to the point where it makes sense to have one horse on which she can compete.

If your child has been involved with horses for some time and you have been active in your child's interest, then you are well aware of the considerable commitment that owning a horse entails. If buying a horse is the right decision for your family, it's strongly recommended that you board him rather than care for him on your own property. Although horses are large, powerful animals, they are deceptively fragile and vulnerable to myriad injuries and illnesses, even from something as seemingly simple as the kind of food they eat and how much of it they are given.

> While leasing a horse can be extremely rewarding for all parties, it can also be a financial and legal nightmare. And never forget that the leased "property" is a living, breathing animal whose health and well-being depend on all the humans involved.

Why You Should Look a Gift Horse in the Mouth

If you are ever offered a free horse, run away. Fast. All horses have some intrinsic value and all horse people know it. Whether it's a few hundred or tens of thousands of dollars, horses are worth money. When someone wants to give away a horse, there's a darned good reason why. For example, people may be willing to give away an ancient horse because the effort to sell the animal just isn't worthwhile. And while the combination of an older horse and a young riding student can

> ## The Horse and Rider Equation
>
> Green Horse + Green Rider = Dangerous Situation
> Green Horse + Experienced Rider = Good Situation
> Experienced Horse + Green Rider = The Best Situation
>
> "Green" describes a horse's or rider's level of training, knowledge, and skill, not their age. Just because a horse is mature, even elderly, does not mean that it can't also be green (untrained) and therefore utterly inappropriate for an inexperienced rider or handler.

work beautifully in the right situation, elderly horses often have special nutritional and medical needs that can equate to greater expenses.

People may also be willing to give away a young horse before much time has been invested in his training. Even more so than with an aged horse, this is a situation to be avoided at all costs. Acquiring a young horse is nothing at all like adopting a puppy or a kitten. It takes a skilled and experienced trainer several years to properly educate a young horse, and a beginning rider should never be put on a partially trained horse.

The Problem with Ponies

It is not uncommon for ponies to be given away as children outgrow them, but they are notorious for having been allowed to develop horrible behavior. Horse people who have had bad experiences with spoiled, bad-tempered, even vicious ponies may avoid all ponies as a result of those experiences. This is a shame, because a pony with good manners and a kind disposition can teach a small, inexperienced rider a great deal, without the intimidating height, strength, and speed of a tall horse.

The reason so many ponies are little monsters is, frankly, the people who own them. Ponies are small and cute, so when they begin to misbehave, people often think it's cute or funny and indulge the lack of manners. Poor behavior tends to spiral downward and become harder and harder to correct as it becomes habitual. Eventually the animal may turn into a confirmed biter, kicker, and/or bucker. It often happens that individuals who own ponies are not experienced with equines — they're parents with a horse-crazy kid or an adult who longed for a horse as a child and never had one, so they purchased what might be called a "yard ornament" or "BYP" (backyard pony).

Sometimes a non-horse person will feel that he or she simply has to man-handle the pony to teach him a lesson, to show him who's boss, and to force the "proper" attitude. And the bad situation only worsens. Eventually, the pony becomes more trouble than he's worth

> The phrase "never look a gift horse in the mouth" probably comes from the practice of determining a horse's age by looking at his teeth.

or the child begins to dislike horses because of the pony's bad behavior. So the parents look around for someone else with a horse-crazy child and the pony goes to a new home, only to continue the cycle.

It is possible to find a gentle, kind pony with superb manners and an excellent disposition, but those individuals who are fortunate enough to have such a pony often keep him for life and won't sell for any amount of money. That's how rare they are!

Kid-Friendly Often Isn't

Expecting the best of others is a terrific trait, but anticipating that someone who is selling a horse meant for a child will be honest in their assessment of the horse's temperament and suitability for a young rider is naive and potentially dangerous. Unfortunately, there are some individuals with horses to sell who will describe those animals in any way necessary to find a buyer. The number of ads in newspapers describing horses as "kid-friendly" could easily lead an inexperienced person to believe that horses with the appropriate training and disposition abound and are simple to find. They aren't and they're not.

While there are many outstanding individuals in the horse world who are, indeed, candid in their straightforward evaluations of their horses' qualities, it can be quite difficult to sort out the people with sterling characters from those who will do or say anything to sell a horse.

Always keep the following in mind: Ponies and horses who are genuinely kind and can be trusted to pack a child around are gems, and few owners will part with them readily. Always ask why an animal described as "kid friendly" is for sale — has the former child owner outgrown the animal, has he or she lost interest in horses, or has the

Selecting a horse for your child doesn't require you to be a horse expert. But you do need advice from trusted and knowledgeable horse people representing you and your child — the seller is not that person!

family's situation changed and they can no longer keep horses? All of these are legitimate reasons to sell a horse or pony.

Finding the Right Horse

The ideal situation is one in which the instructor is your partner in finding the best, suitable, safest, kindest horse possible for your child. Chances are good that one exists in the barn where she rides, perhaps even her favorite lesson horse. Your instructor not only has expertise with horses but also knowledge of your child's skill level, personality, and confidence. She has contacts in the local horse world and more than likely has considerable experience buying horses of her own.

If you do locate a horse on your own that you think might be suitable, involve your child's instructor in examining the horse. You will want her evaluation not only of the horse himself but also her advice on how to incorporate a new horse into your child's ongoing lessons.

A Word to the Wise

Although newspaper ads and online resources can provide good leads to potential horses, don't be tempted to buy a horse at an auction. Prospective buyers know nothing of the horse's background, his disposition, his health, or his training, and you don't have the time necessary to make a considered decision. Only an experienced horse person has the skills and experience necessary to deal with whatever they might buy at auction.

Novice owners should also avoid rescue situations. It can be enormously tempting to "save" a neglected or abused horse; however, most horses in difficult circumstances require a great deal of rehab, retraining, and medical care to become solid citizens. As with an auction, you have no way of knowing what issues the horse may bring along.

And finally, never buy a horse that is listed as a "prospect" — this means that the horse has the potential talent or disposition to perform in a particular discipline but not the training or experience. Don't even consider looking at horses with descriptions that read "intermediate rider" or have any other language that makes you question the horse's disposition or dependability for a beginning rider.

The Behavior Check

Once you have identified a possible match, insist on visiting the animal and ask the seller to handle the horse or pony for you so you can watch. You'll want to see the animal's reaction to having his legs and feet handled, to being groomed and led around, to having his face and ears rubbed, and to being saddled. Watch for any telltale signs of resentment or fear — ears pinned, whites showing around the eyes, trying to evade the handler, a hitched hip (threatening a kick), lashing tail, pawing the ground, spooking sideways, or flinching.

Also watch how the handler interacts with the animal — is he or she kind and gentle or abrupt and rough? Does the handler seem genuinely fond of the horse or pony, or indifferent to his feelings and reactions?

If everything looks good so far, ask some questions: What activities did the former child owner do with the animal? Trail riding, play days, horse shows, lessons? Are there photos or videos of these activities? Ask for the former rider to climb up on the animal so you can see how well he responds; watch him move and get a feel for his behavior under saddle. If the seller is hesitant, you need to ask why. If the child has become frightened of riding, of course you would never insist that he or she ride for you or allow an adult to force them to. But you do need to explore why the fear exists — did something happen with this animal that has made the former child owner afraid?

And you need to ask some tough, direct questions (and hope you'll hear some direct, honest replies): Has the animal ever bucked or reared? Does he bite or strike? Does he crib or chew wood? Very

Maintaining Objectivity

Although your child should be involved in the purchase process, be aware of the danger that one or the other of you (or both!) might fall in love with a particular horse before determining his suitability. Your child's age and maturity should guide your decision on this issue, but it might be best for you and your instructor to narrow down your choices to several true possibilities before taking your child to visit any of them.

Once you've determined that a horse is a candidate, your instructor and then your child should handle him, tack him up, and ride him before a final decision is made. Making two or three visits to several different horses may seem like a huge hassle, but keep in mind that you are making a long-term commitment; it makes sense to take as much time as you need to make the right choice. You and your child will also learn a lot about horses from this process, so view the whole experience as time well spent.

few boarding stables will allow horses or ponies with these habits because they destroy every flat surface they can reach.

A word about observing the disposition of horses you visit — you must always be on the alert for the possibility that the horse has been drugged. Again, just because a horse seller knows that an animal may become the mount of a child does not mean that person will not do anything it takes to sell the horse. The saying "buyer beware" goes double for anyone buying a horse, and you cannot trust in the seller's integrity or good intentions. This is why several visits to see the horse — at least one with your child's instructor — as well as a vet check are so critical.

> A horse without shoes is said to be barefoot. Though the majority of horses are shod, many horses can be ridden perfectly well without shoes, and interest in "natural hoof care" is growing.

The Unofficial Health Check

If the horse or pony being considered passes muster on the behavior front, the next questions should be about the horse or pony's health regimen and feeding schedule. Here are some examples of issues to think about.

How often is the horse dewormed? This may depend on what part of the country you live in — in areas with freezing winters, deworming regimens differ from those with year-round parasites. Your main concern is to learn if the animal has been on a regular schedule of parasite control.

What has his vaccination schedule been? Again, this will vary regionally, but it's important to determine if the animal has received regular vaccinations as appropriate for your area.

What is he fed and how much? Is he used to grazing in a pasture for some or all of the day, or is he given only hay? What about grain or other concentrated feed?

Does he receive any nutritional supplements? If so, what for? What is the monthly cost of the supplements?

The Official Vet Check

If everything still looks and sounds positive, you need to arrange for an official vet check. This can seem a little challenging, as you may not know any horse vets, but your instructor can assist you in finding one. You may be tempted to have the owner's vet perform the inspection, but this is generally not encouraged.

The issue isn't a question of the vet's integrity, but rather, a concern about putting him or her in a tough spot — performing a vet check on a client's horse. If the vet finds something that kills the purchase, the client may not react well and the vet could potentially lose his business. Finding another vet, therefore, is both a courtesy and a chance to have a neutral evaluation.

From Toe to Head

There's an old saying in the horse world: "No foot, no horse." When you're examining a potential purchase, look very carefully at his feet. Does he wear horseshoes? Just on the front feet or all four? What is the reasoning? Horses are traditionally shod to protect their hooves when they are being ridden consistently, especially on hard surfaces, but in many cases, it's because the feet are prone to chipping or splitting.

Ask how often the farrier trims the animal's hooves and what kind of shoes he has — you'll probably want to avoid a horse or pony who needs complicated hoof care. In looking at the animal's feet, what impression do you get? You can simply observe them, standing next to the pony. Do they look neat and tidy, well cared for? Or are they long, cracked, or ragged on the edges?

Be particularly wary if the animal's hooves curl up at the tips — this is a horse or pony whose feet have been neglected for some time and whose owner has not performed the most basic form of care. What else has the owner skimped on?

If your vet finds a problem, you can ask him or her to contact the regular vet and discuss the issue (with the owner's permission, of course) to see if there's a history and/or if minor intervention would resolve it. After conferring, your vet would have a better picture of the situation and be better able to advise you.

By the way, if the seller doesn't have a regular vet, you should be concerned, as it probably means the pony has not received regular care — no vaccinations, no deworming, no annual Coggins (a simple blood test done once a year to ensure the animal does not have Equine Infectious Anemia, a viral disease for which there is no vaccination and no cure). If you are going to board the pony, no respectable boarding stable will allow an equine on its property without a negative Coggins.

The Purchase Agreement

If you decide to go ahead with the purchase, be sure the purchase agreement thoroughly outlines all details related to the horse or pony. This includes a description — gender, color, age, height, breed, microchip number (if any), and breed association and registry number (if applicable — keep in mind that non-registered "grade" horses and ponies make some of the best children's mounts). The purchase price and any conditions related to it should be clearly outlined, especially if you are making payments over a period of time and not purchasing the horse or pony outright.

The seller should provide you with a signed statement that the animal is in good health, that the seller is the legal owner, and that no encumbrances prohibit the sale of the animal. If you are purchasing the horse or pony over a period of time, making regular payments, you need to work out details related to the animal's upkeep (vet, farrier, board) during the time you're paying the purchase price, as well as removal of the animal — typically, you can't take possession until all payments have been made to the seller.

Some individuals will include in their contract a statement regarding the buyer's intent to provide all necessary upkeep for the animal for the period of time the buyer owns him (basically, you'll take care of it), and many contracts will also include a "buy back" statement that gives the seller first right of refusal if you ever decide to sell the horse or pony.

In summary, remember that a purchase agreement is a legal contract. You should consider obtaining the advice of an attorney before signing. Getting the input of a knowledgeable horse person can also be terrifically useful, as most will be very familiar with details that could be considered "standard" and will notice anything out of the ordinary.

CRAZY ABOUT HORSES

I have always loved horses! I draw horses all the time; horses are my hobby. I love them because they are nice and caring, and I love my lesson horse because he takes care of me. Riding makes me feel confident. I want to have a big horse with brown and white splotches on it.

— *Cameron*, age 8

My advice is to let them ride if they want to. It teaches responsibility, kindness, and respect. Riding has been wonderful for Cameron. Her instructor is amazing. She fuels Cameron's desire to improve and make it "her thing." No one else in our family rides and we were resistant to the idea initially, but I just started taking lessons myself and I love it!

— *Jaclyn*, Cameron's mom

8

You Bought a Horse — Now What?

As mentioned earlier, the best option for a first-time horse owner is to board the horse rather than care for him solely on your own. And the best place to board the horse is at your child's lesson barn. Owning and caring for a horse on a daily basis is nothing like owning a dog or cat — there is an enormous amount to learn about horses' surprising delicacy and vulnerability to injury and illness before attempting to keep a horse on one's own property.

For example, did you know that too much grass can be bad for horses? That they need their hooves trimmed every six to eight weeks? That they need the companionship of other animals, preferably horses? That they don't do well being kept in a stall most of the time and need room to move around? Not to sound like the voice of doom, but horse people are all too well aware that most horses could find a way to hurt themselves even in a padded cell! If you're just starting out in horse ownership, you, your child, and your horse will benefit from the guidance of experienced barn owners.

Talking the Talk

Farrier. The person who trims hooves and puts shoes on horses.

Deworming. Treating a horse for parasites; a necessary component of horse health.

Box stall. A stall that is large enough (usually 12' × 12') for a horse to move around and lie down in.

Tie stall. A narrow stall where the horse is haltered and tied; used for feeding and grooming but not suitable for a horse to stay in for long periods of time.

What Horses Need

When you are looking for a boarding facility for a horse, even when considering your child's lesson barn as the most viable option, you need to consider three basic needs: food, shelter, and safety. Horses evolved to eat most of the day while in constant motion — grazing horses take a bite of grass and move a step or two for the next bite of grass, taking breaks to drink, nap, or play. A wild herd can easily cover 30 to 40 miles a day. As a consequence, equines need room to move around freely. Remaining in a stall all day can lead to extreme behavioral problems and to poor health.

> There are three basic truths about owning a horse:
> 1. Horses are always hungry.
> 2. Poop happens and happens and happens.
> 3. If there's a way for a horse to hurt himself, he will.

The ideal situation is one where your horse will have several hours of outdoor turnout every day (the more the better), even if he is unable to graze. Maintaining enough pasture to allow a large group of horses to graze is difficult, so most horses are fed hay at least twice a day and most receive some sort of concentrated feed in the form of grain as well, though this is not always necessary if sufficient hay is provided.

Horses are also highly social animals and must have companionship, which is another good reason to choose a boarding facility rather than keeping your horse at home. Horses who live alone, even with a loving and attentive owner, are usually lonely, unhappy, and nervous. The ideal companion is another horse or pony, or even a donkey. Goats can also make good companions for horses. At a barn, your horse will most likely be turned out with other horses or will at least be able to see and smell them around him at all times.

The Cost of Keeping a Horse

If you're considering buying a horse, you need to have an idea of some of the costs involved. The basics are the same as any other creature needs for survival: food, water, shelter. Depending on where you live, the cost of basic feed, hay, vet, and farrier bills can differ widely: high cost-of-living areas have higher horse expenses, while metropolitan areas will have fewer horse-friendly services and choices close at hand. Here are some examples of standard expenses related to horse upkeep:

Item	Price Range
Hay (grass)	$6.50–$12.50 (per 70-pound square bale)
Feed (crimped oats)	$10.50–$14.50 (per 40-pound bag)
Shavings (bedding)	$5.50–$9.50 (per 60-pound compressed bale)
Vet: barn call	$35–$85 (to drive to the barn)
Vet: emergency	$100–$150 (to drive to the barn after hours)
Annual vaccinations	$150–$350
Deworming program	$8–$15 (per tube, monthly or quarterly)
Farrier: trim only	$35–$85 (every 6 weeks or so)
Farrier: plain shoes	$75–$150 (all four feet, every 6 weeks or so)
Full board (stall provided)	$300–$800 and up (per month, including feed)
Pasture board (no stall)	$200–$500 and up (per month, including feed)

The expenses listed above are just the basics — standard upkeep essential for keeping a horse healthy. If the worst happens and a horse becomes seriously ill or injured, vet bills can quickly skyrocket into the thousands. Other expenses include equipment such as tack, halter and lead rope, blankets (if used), and grooming tools.

Types of Board

Horses can be boarded with either "full care" or "pasture board" (also called "rough board"). Full care usually includes a stall (ideally for nighttime and foul weather use) and turnout time (the more the better), as well as access to the arena(s), grooming area(s), wash rack(s), and other facilities.

Pasture board usually means that the horse is kept in a pasture or paddock 24 hours a day, with some sort of shelter for inclement weather but no stall. Some pasture-board farms may have a few stalls available, should you want to use one temporarily while working with your horse or for health care purposes; but the horses are not brought in and stalled on a routine basis.

In both cases, the horses are monitored regularly and fed — usually twice daily — and have access to fresh water. A horse's diet varies considerably depending on its size, age, condition, and the amount of work it's doing, but you can expect an average horse to eat as much as a bale of hay a day if no grass is available. Grain requirements can range from none at all to several quarts a day. Full care is the most expensive, with pasture board a decent alternative offered by some facilities.

A third option that can sometimes be found is "self-care" in which the owner is required to go out and perform all of the horse care — which means checking the horses and feeding twice a day, morning and evening, and ensuring access to water. It is the least expensive, but the most labor-intensive, option for owners.

Evaluating Boarding Facilities

Ideally, you would keep a leased or purchased horse at the barn where your child is already taking lessons. Most likely, your child's instructor would help locate a suitable horse or pony for your child's level of experience and her personality and interests. If, for some reason, you choose to board the animal at another facility, you would employ the same characteristics you used to gauge the lesson barn, with the added element of the animal's safety and well-being. Things that create a hazard to the horse or pony also create a hazard to those working with or around that horse or pony — specifically, your child.

Looking at Barns

Barns come in many shapes and sizes, but the key components are for them to be safe, solid, and healthy for the horses (that is, provide adequate light, ventilation, and shelter), and safe for people to interact with and around the horses. As a boarder, you should look for features that meet your and your child's needs, too. Three of the more common types of barns are:

Center aisle (the barn is enclosed and has an aisle that runs down the center, onto which stalls open) — a useful design in areas that regularly experience inclement weather.

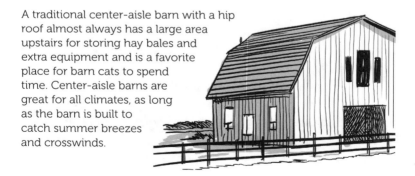

A traditional center-aisle barn with a hip roof almost always has a large area upstairs for storing hay bales and extra equipment and is a favorite place for barn cats to spend time. Center-aisle barns are great for all climates, as long as the barn is built to catch summer breezes and crosswinds.

Shedrow barns are a good choice in warmer climates, where the sheltered aisle is open to the outside. This design allows for excellent air circulation and gives the stabled horses an interesting view of the outside world.

Shedrow (a row of stalls opens to a covered walkway and the outdoors) — a useful design in areas that have mostly temperate weather.

Pole barn (open-air construction, with poles supporting the roof and acting as dividers between stalls) — a design ideally suited to arid, very hot climates.

Why is it useful to you, as a parent and prospective boarder, to be aware of barn styles? Because the barn can tell you a great deal about the facility, and its design, uses, and upkeep can create an environment of relative safety — or hazard — for your child.

While many owners buy property on which the barn is already built and, consequently, have no say in the design of the barn, the use to which the owner puts the barn and the design's flexibility to support that use will be very important to you — again, because your child will also be using it. Here are some of the features you should look at.

EXAMINE THE AISLES

How wide are the barn aisles? With horses and people regularly moving through them, they almost can't be wide enough, although 14 feet is a decent width. Look at the flooring. If the aisle is concrete, is the material scored to give horses good traction? Or is it slick, which could be dangerous when the concrete becomes wet? If the aisle is dirt, is it regularly moistened with water to reduce the amount of dust in the air? Or to the other extreme, is drainage a problem? Does water seep in, creating a muddy mess?

You also need to consider the way the space is used. Are horses tied in the aisle for grooming and tacking up? If so, how? There are two ways to tie a horse: cross-tied and head-tied. *Cross-tied* means that the horse stands directly in the center of the aisle with lines connecting the halter to heavy-duty bolts in the walls on either side. This style of tying horses prevents traffic from flowing up and down the aisle.

Head-tied means that the horse is tied with a single line, which allows him to swing his haunches from side to side. Head-tied horses allow traffic to move up and down the aisle, but the practice can create a hazard if the horse is skittish or inclined to kick. It's not always possible, but ideally aisles should not be used for tying horses at all — there should be a grooming area, separate from the aisle, where horses can be tied for grooming and tacking up.

Finally, notice if the aisle is tidy and well maintained. Is it regularly swept and free of manure? Is it used for storage of hay bales, tack trunks, and wheelbarrows? Even tractors? Preferably, aisles are kept utterly clear of everything — the less stuff there is in the way, the safer the area is for both horse and handler.

When You've Got to Go

The location of the bathroom is a surprisingly important consideration in selecting a barn. Is it conveniently located in the barn or is it a hike down the lane to another building? Is there even a bathroom available? If there is just a portable toilet, are you and your child comfortable using it? If not, where will you have to take your child should she need to use the rest room? The owner's on-site home, if he or she will allow it? A local gas station?

Study the Stalls

The standard size for a box stall is 12 × 12 feet, which provides enough room for the average horse to move around comfortably and lie down safely. In some facilities you might see "tie stalls" that are designed for horses to stand facing a wall with their heads tied to a ring. These may be used for feeding horses who live outdoors most of the time or for grooming and tacking up. They are not adequate for animals to spend more than an hour or two at a time in.

> Once your child is skilled and confident enough to work outside the arena, it would be a bonus to have riding trails on the property to practice her skills in a new setting. Both horses and riders benefit from a change of scenery!

There are two basic types of bedding used commonly in stalls: shavings and straw. Shavings can come in a variety of thicknesses, from almost sawdust to bigger slices of wood. Of the two types of bedding, shavings are usually easier for horse facilities to manage, as they're easy to sift through for solid waste and wet material, which allows for more economical cleaning of stalls. Straw is generally cheaper to buy, but because it's harder to manage and to clean, the barn may have greater labor expenses and waste. What is most important is that the bedding be changed regularly.

Check out the Storage Buildings

As a boarder, you don't need a great deal of knowledge about storage buildings, other than to understand their very basic purpose and the utility of having available storage. Depending on the size of the boarding facility, the number of horses, and the amount of equipment the property owner has, having outbuildings for storage can be extremely helpful and can actually save money, as it allows the owner to purchase supplies such as shavings and hay in bulk. This in turn benefits you by keeping overall costs down. As well, storage buildings ensure that supplies and equipment will not be stored in barn aisles, which helps to keep those aisles open and clear for your child to move through.

Looking at the Land

As a prospective boarder, there are several considerations to keep in mind when you look at the overall size of the property. Because your child is still learning to ride and should be in a suitable arena while mounted, the amount of acreage is not a major concern. The condition of that land, however, is something to consider as you gauge the overall professionalism of the boarding facility and the staff's attention to maintenance and upkeep. Here are some questions to ask:

- If the facility has horses in pastures, how many are in each?

What's a Loafing Shed?

If you choose pasture or rough board for your horse (see box, page 132), you will not be concerned with the stalls in the barn, but you should take a close look at the outdoor shelter your horse will have access to. Horses can tolerate fairly wide extremes in weather conditions and often seem to prefer being outside in the rain and snow. However, they must be able to escape harsh sun and severe weather such as hail; hard, cold rain; and icy winds. A properly situated three-side loafing shed or run-in provides adequate protection from all but the most extreme weather.

Loafing sheds must be large enough to accommodate the number of horses who need shelter, as dominant horses may prevent submissive horses from coming under cover. It's also not unknown for a dominant horse to corner a more submissive pasture mate inside a loafing shed and kick him mercilessly, so the building should either be completely open on one side or have several exits so that horses can escape. This is an added safety feature for inexperienced handlers, including children, who may enter a loafing shed to halter a horse and need an easy and quick way to get out if the horses begin jostling or kicking.

- Do horses have enough room to move around or do they appear to be crowded?
- What does the land look like in the pastures? Is it covered in green and lush grass? Or are there chest-high weeds with patches of bare dirt?
- If horses are kept in dry lots (paddocks without grass), is the ground sandy and clean? Or is it hard-packed dirt with heavily pocked holes in it, created by horses having to walk on it after hard rains?
- Do the paddocks have hazards like rocks, tree trunks, or fallen limbs lying around in them?
- Is the pasture covered in manure, fresh and old? Or does it appear to be cleaned regularly?
- Do the water sources (troughs, automatic waterers, or buckets) hold enough for several thirsty horses to have as much as they want? How clean are the containers and the water?
- If there is a pond, is it clean and clear or is it scummy and covered in thick algae?

A boarding facility doesn't need a huge amount of land — a barn, an indoor arena, a limited number of small turnout paddocks, and a storage building or two could easily fit on five to six acres, if designed thoughtfully. A more important factor is the quality and usability of the acreage. Forty acres of land is a lot, but if most of it is rocky or extremely hilly, it's not very useful for keeping horses.

But generally, as a boarder, so long as there is a safe arena in which your child can ride, you won't really care too much about the size of the property. As in all things, the key is the condition of that property and the effort the owner puts into maintaining it.

Looking at Fences

Fences are a big deal for an equine facility, and they are something you should look at carefully when you inspect a barn. In most cases, they are solid, immovable elements your child will interact with every time she rides or interacts with a horse there. In other situations, the fence lines may change as horses are rotated to different pastures and new areas are marked out with electric tape. The style of fence and its condition are key to your child's safety. Here are some other reasons a good fence is of critical concern:

Fences must contain the horses effectively — if your horse gets loose and is hurt or, worse, hurts someone else, you may have some liability in the situation, especially if the horse has gotten loose more than once (some horses are true escape artists!).

Fences must be sturdy enough to limit the amount of damage a horse can do to himself — an injured horse costs money and can't be ridden. Fences must be constructed to limit the amount of damage a horse can inflict on it — if your horse damages the facility owner's fences, you may be required to pay for repairs.

Fences must create an adequate barrier between horses in different paddocks. Horses can hurt each other or even knock fences down while fighting or playing. Having solid perimeter fencing on the property is also critical.

> Property owners spend a fortune (not to mention a lot of physical effort) to maintain their fences. Children (or adults!) climbing on the fences or swinging on the gates can damage fences pretty quickly.

Remember: The fences often provide the first impression a visitor has of the property. So how the property owners maintain fences says a lot about their approach to overall facilities maintenance and attention to detail. Shoddy care for their fences can often mean shoddy care elsewhere. Be on the lookout for sagging or broken boards, dangling wires, leaning fence posts, and the like.

Fencing Hazards to Look Out For

Barbed wire fences are durable, inexpensive, and not too difficult to put up. The jagged barbs, however, can do serious damage to horses, especially if they become tangled in it. Also, as the barbed wire ages, it can rust and easily break into brittle sections — it becomes very difficult to work with at that point and is more of a hazard. This is not a good choice of fence for horses and children to be around.

PVC board looks attractive, but it is lightweight and easily damaged. An overexcited horse can break right through it.

T-posts are everywhere, primarily because they are extremely durable, relatively inexpensive and versatile — virtually any kind of horizontal fencing element can be attached to them. With their sharp ends, however, T-posts can be dangerous for horses and for riders if, heaven forbid, they should fall onto the post. For safety reasons, please make sure the property owner has covered the tops of the T-posts with plastic caps.

Horse Tack, Equipment, and Supplies

Once you purchase a horse or pony, your child will need tack and equipment in order to handle and ride the animal. It is extremely important that you seek knowledgeable assistance in this effort and not try to figure out proper fit yourself — a poorly fitted bit, bridle, or saddle can hurt a horse, and even the gentlest animal will react to pain in such a way that your child might be put at risk.

Choosing the right bit is particularly important; a harsh bit can cause serious damage to the tender gum tissues and tongue, creating severe enough pain to cause some animals to rear and even throw themselves over backward in an effort to escape the agony in his mouth. Other bits, while not harsh in and of themselves, can work on something of a pulley system and create pressure on the top of the horse's head. An animal not accustomed to this sensation could become quite frightened and react badly to the strange feeling.

It's critical to know what type of tack the horse is accustomed to. It's no big deal to change a cat's collar or to introduce a dog to the leash, but horses and ponies can be rather sensitive and react badly to strange sensations and new things. Being aware of this, as well as having a basic understanding of the equipment used for horseback riding, can only help your child and serve to ensure her continued safety.

Finding the Proper Bridle

Bridles are usually sold as three separate components: the headstall, the reins, and the bit. They are typically made of leather but are also available in synthetic materials. It is correct to have the same color bridle as the saddle; for example, a dark brown bridle with a dark brown saddle. The bridle must be correctly fitted to the horse or pony and must suit the rider's needs and discipline interests.

An English bridle can be identified by its more complex design: In addition to the band of leather that attaches to the bit and goes over the top of the horse's head to attach to the other side of the bit, it is composed of a brow band (which goes across the horse's forehead), a throat latch (which goes under the horse's cheeks or jowls), and a cavesson or noseband (which wraps around the horse's face, above the nostrils). The advantage to all of these bands is that the bridle cannot easily slip over the horse's ears and come off.

English bridle

Western bridles are quite simple in their design, with a single strap that attaches to either side of the bit and goes behind the horse's ears. Other designs include a loop around one or both of the horse's ears. Still other designs may have a throatlatch that goes under the horse's cheeks.

Western bridle

CRAZY ABOUT HORSES

When I was two, I used to answer the door blowing air through my lips because that's how horses greet each other. Horses don't care if you're mentally or physically challenged or about the color of your skin. They'll stay true to you no matter what.

I lease a pony named Jay, but I dream of owning a dapple-grey Thoroughbred. I will name him Trix R4 Kids or So Much for Luv. He will be an excellent eventer/jumper and we will go to the top. I love Jay, though. He's trustworthy, loving, and he follows me around like a puppy. He's the best and kindest little dude on the farm.

— *Audria*, age 15

My daughter is definitely "horse crazy." She is always either at the barn or reading about horses and horsemanship. Her interest in horses has allowed her to meet many wonderful people, given her an opportunity to be physically active, and taught her a great deal about animal training and care. I spend a lot of time at the barn, but I also spend a lot of time with her, which is good.

— *Kathy*, Audria's mom

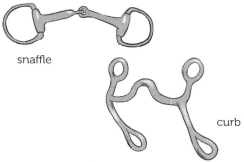

snaffle

curb

Finding the Proper Bit

Even experienced horse people sometimes feel bewildered when facing a wall covered with hundreds of bits at the tack shop. Fortunately, most horse owners don't need to know all the nuances of bit selection and materials used. But it is helpful to have a feel for some of the basic types that might be of use to your child.

THE SNAFFLE BIT

The snaffle bit is the most common type of bit in English riding. The typical snaffle bit comprises a hinged metal piece, called the port, with rings on each end that connect the bit to the bridle and the reins. When the rider pulls on the reins, the snaffle works by applying direct pressure on the horse's gums behind his teeth (this area is called the bars). The simplest style of ring for a snaffle is probably the D-ring, so named because the rings are in the shape of a capital "D." Loose-ring snaffles have circular rings that spin and can pinch the horse's lips as they rotate, so it is critical that the bit be wide enough for the horse's mouth.

The snaffle should be made of smooth metal or rubber of a reasonable thickness to fit into the horse's mouth comfortably. A thicker bit is gentler but can be uncomfortable for the horse if it is too thick. A very thin bit (thinner than your index finger) or one made of twisted metal is quite severe and should not be used.

The Curb Bit

Just as with English bits, Western bits are available in an astonishing variety of styles. The most basic design, the curb or Quarter Horse bit, is a solid piece of metal (the bar or port) connected to the two side arms (called cheeks or shanks). It may also have a chinstrap or curb chain that runs under the horse's

Ways to Save

Horse people have become very wise about finding ways to save money, and purchasing tack is no exception. Talk first with your child's instructor to see if he or she has any well-cared-for tack that would fit your child's horse or pony, and if the instructor would be willing to sell it. It's also possible that boarders in the barn might have gently used tack you could buy.

Many tack stores offer a consignment section in which horse people display their used tack for sale. You can be fairly confident of the quality found in most tack shops' selection of consignment tack because they will want tack that is only slightly worn and still structurally sound.

If with the help of your instructor you can determine what sizes of bit, saddle, girth, and so on your horse needs, you can check online sites (see Resources for Parents) for "starter tack sets." The savings can be significant compared with purchasing items individually, and most companies have customer service representatives who are usually experienced horse people themselves and can offer knowledgeable assistance over the phone.

Always have a horse person's assistance to help you ensure a proper fit for your child's horse or pony. Bridles, bits, saddles, and girths — whether English or Western — are never "one size fits all." It's imperative for your child's safety that the equipment she uses is appropriate to the animal.

jaw. The port is usually slightly rounded toward the roof of the horse's mouth, which means that it is contoured to the shape of the tongue and is more comfortable than a solid bar of metal lying straight and flat across.

A curb bit works by applying pressure to the bars of the mouth, the chin, and the poll (behind the ears). The longer the side arms, the more severe the action of the port. Because it can produce greater pressure than a snaffle, a curb bit is more appropriately used by an experienced rider, as it may injure a horse's mouth if not used properly.

Finding the Proper Saddle

Whether English or Western, the first, most critical fit is for the horse; the second, for the rider. Because of where a saddle sets on the horse, the width of the saddle affects the movement of the shoulders, as well as how the horse carries the rider — over the horse's center of gravity (which is correct), or too far forward (which unbalances the horse) or too far back (which can put the rider's weight painfully over the horse's kidneys, as well as affect his balance). A saddletree (the central structure that balances the saddle along the spine) that is too narrow can pinch the

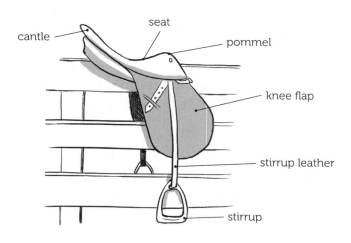

English saddle

horse's shoulders and make movement uncomfortable, and one that's too wide can cause painful rubbing, much as a shoe that is too large will give you blisters.

If the saddle is positioned incorrectly on the horse's back, the rider's position and balance can also be affected negatively, so it's important that a correctly fitted saddle be placed properly on the horse.

The Western saddle's design is a natural for inexperienced riders — the horn on the front of the saddle, traditionally used to attach a lariat or rope, makes a wonderful handle to grab, and the greater size and deeper seat can help a rider feel more secure. English saddles can be made more "friendly" for inexperienced riders by attaching a leather strap to the D-rings (D-shaped rings on the front side of the saddle, up near the top) that a rider could hold on to if need be. These straps are often referred to as "bucking straps," a pretty self-explanatory description of their basic purpose.

For the very young rider, a variation of the English saddle is the "lead line" design. This is, essentially, an English saddle with a strap built into the front of the saddle, where little hands can easily and naturally hold on. These saddles tend to be pretty "deep,"

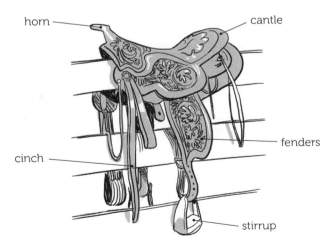

horn

cantle

fenders

cinch

stirrup

Western saddle

meaning that the saddle embraces the rider's seat more fully through its extended front and back design. And that deepness provides an added sense of security and balance to riders as they develop their skill and confidence in the saddle.

With either an English or Western saddle, a saddle pad (English) or saddle blanket (Western) is placed between the saddle and the horse's back. Both pads and blankets come in a wide variety of colors and thickness, as well as styles. The key is to find one that fits the horse or pony and that will provide adequate cushioning and protection from the friction created between the horse's (often sweaty) back and the underside of the saddle. (And buy two, because they need to be washed!)

With the exception of competing in English horse shows with traditional rules for tack, saddle pads and blankets can provide a fun opportunity for your child to express her own personal style with bright colors, flashy patterns, and even tassels.

Wait, There's More!

Yes, it is possible to run amok in a tack store and buy all kinds of gear for both horse and rider; but once you have purchased properly fitting tack, there is little equipment that you absolutely must have. Depending on your climate, a winter blanket may be desirable, though horses can live quite happily without them, given sufficient shelter. It makes sense to wait and see what is needed (a fly mask in the summer, for example), rather than rushing out and buying one of everything you see.

Basic Barn Gear

Every horse must have his own halter and lead rope so that people can handle him on the ground, lead him, or tie him. Halters are usually made of either leather or nylon, with nylon being the more economical (and longer lasting) choice. Leather is generally considered safer, however, especially if your horse is turned out with his halter on, as is a frequent practice at some boarding barns. Leather will break if the horse becomes caught on a fence post or even puts his own foot through the straps (it happens!). If you do prefer a nylon halter, buy one with a breakaway strap. It is always best to remove the halter before turning the horse loose.

Lead lines can be found in leather, nylon, or cotton rope and come in a variety of lengths. Some versions have a piece of chain between the snap and the line itself; the chain can be wrapped around the horse's nose if he is difficult to lead. A child shouldn't be handling such a horse, anyway, and the chain can whack a horse on the chin if left to dangle, so this style is best left on the shelf.

Many horse people believe that cotton lead ropes are the most economical and easiest to use — unlike nylon, cotton won't burn your hands as badly in the event that a horse pulls away or bolts. They're also easier to tie and untie, which is especially important for small hands. But, which material to use may ultimately be a simple matter of personal preference.

Gathering a Grooming Kit

The basics needed for a grooming kit are a dandy brush (a stiff body brush), a soft brush for the face and legs, a currycomb for tackling muddy clumps, a brush or comb for the mane and tail, and a hoof pick. It's a great deal of fun to find supplies that match the color of the carrier, or your child could choose to have a full rainbow of colors. There are plenty of other delightful items that could be purchased for the grooming kit, if you're inclined — tack stores and farm feed stores are filled with them and any salesperson would be happy to help you and your child find even more — but your child will be suitably equipped with this small collection.

A basic grooming kit can be kept in a plastic container that has interior sections and a handle for easy carrying. Labeling each item with the horse's name is a good idea.

Safely Tying a Horse or Pony

Tying is not just a matter of finding a fence post or sturdy wall hardware and tying a knot with the lead rope. In fact, it would almost be better to leave the horse standing with a loose and hanging lead rope than to tie him with a regular knot. If the horse panics and pulls against the rope, his reaction will typically be to pull even harder, making the knot impossible to untie. And then, the only way to free the horse is to cut the lead rope — a dangerous proposition, as this requires stepping close to a thrashing horse with a sharp knife in your hand.

That's why horse people use a "quick-release" knot — a slip knot that can be quickly disengaged by tugging on the hanging end, even if the horse is fighting against the rope. This releases the pressure on the horse's head and, often, immediately calms him (it's the pressure and feeling trapped that can panic some horses). Even with a safety knot in place, however, an inexperienced handler, especially a child, should not attempt to release a horse who is struggling to free himself. It's just too dangerous.

More Ways to Save

In addition to purchasing gently used tack, you have the option to buy tack made of synthetic material (English or Western) instead of the more expensive leather traditionally used in riding equipment. At one time, synthetics were viewed unfavorably, but this has gradually changed as some of the world's finest equestrians have begun using synthetic tack themselves.

There are a number of synthetic options available; Wintec is one of the better known. Regardless of the manufacturer, the advantages of synthetic tack are plentiful: it's weather resistant, comes in a variety of surfaces (for example, sueded for extra "stick" in the saddle), is offered in different colors, and is very attractive. It's also extremely durable and easy to care for, unlike leather, which can be easily damaged and requires regular attention to keep it clean and in good condition. Many synthetic styles, and some leather models, also have sizing options that allow a single saddle to be fitted to a variety of horses, unlike traditional leather saddles that typically fit a single horse.

Glossary

Aids. How a rider or handler tells the horse what she wants him to do. For example, the rider tells the horse to go faster by squeezing with her legs.

Appaloosa. A breed of horse with a pattern of small, distinctive spots on his coat. The breed has two primary genetic color patterns: Leopard (small spots all over) and Blanket (spots concentrated over the rump and back).

Balanced seat. No matter the discipline, the goal of all riding is to have a balanced seat. This means that the rider is supple, poised, and uses just enough leg to preserve balance while on the horse.

Bald-faced. A horse whose face is mostly white, while the rest of his body is a different color.

Barn sour. A horse that is reluctant to leave the barn and can be difficult to take out on a trail.

Bars. The toothless, gummed section in a horse's mouth where the bit rests.

Bascule. Pronounced "bas-KEWL"; this refers to the arc a horse makes as he goes over a jump. A horse who does not bascule jumps "flat," so that his back is a stiff, straight line rather than a lovely, rounded arc.

Bay. A reddish brown or brown coat with black points (the lower legs, muzzle, mane, and tail). Bays can have some white markings on their faces and on their extreme lower legs.

Bell boots. Made of either leather or rubber, these protective devices fit over the horse's hooves and around the pastern, and are held in place by Velcro or straps. The purpose is to protect a horse's front heels from being damaged by his back hooves when he overreaches.

Billets. Two to three straps, usually made of leather or synthetic material, to which the girth is buckled on an English saddle. On a Western saddle, the billet performs the same function but is a single, long strap (and the girth is called a "cinch").

Bit. The mouthpiece that goes into the horse's mouth and rests on the bars. The bit is attached to both the bridle and the reins, and it helps the rider to turn and to stop the horse. Bits can be made of several types of metal, rubber, polymer, or a combination. They come in a wide variety of styles and sizes, fulfilling many purposes.

Bitless bridle. A bridle that does not have a bit. Hackamores and bosals are two types of bitless bridles.

Blaze. A long, wide white stripe that extends down a horse's face from his forehead to around his muzzle.

Box stall. A stall that is large enough (usually 12' × 12') for a horse to move around and lie down in.

Breast plate. The leather straps that go across the front of a horse's chest and attach to the saddle. The purpose of a breast plate (or breast band, in Western) is to help stabilize the saddle and prevent it from slipping backward.

Bridle. The equipment that goes on a horse's head so the rider can control his movement with the reins.

Buckskin. The color of tanned deer hide. Shades may vary from yellow to dark gold. Points (mane, tail, legs) can be dark brown or black.

Canter. In English riding, the three-beat gait between a trot and a gallop. In Western riding, this is called the lope.

Cantle. The back of the saddle, whether English or Western.

Cavaletti. Poles that are raised off the ground, usually three to six inches, and used to help prepare horses and riders for jumping.

Chestnut. A coppery-red body coat with the mane and tail the same color or lighter. Typically, English riders call this color "chestnut" and Western riders call it "sorrel."

Cinch. The band on a Western saddle that goes under the belly and is fastened in place to keep the saddle on the horse. On an English saddle, this strap is called a "girth."

Coggins test. An annual blood test to check for Equine Infectious Anemia, a highly contagious and often fatal disease. Before transporting an animal from one property to another, to a horse show, or across state lines, a negative Coggins is required.

Colic. Because horses cannot vomit, gastric upset can lead to colic — a painful and potentially fatal condition for a horse. Colicked horses display signs of abdominal pain such as pawing, biting at their sides, rolling, groaning, and profuse sweating. Colic can be caused by a variety of things, including eating too much grain.

Collection. When a horse assumes a rounded, more agile and balanced posture, which takes a certain degree of fitness and training. A horse can be collected at all gaits.

Colt. A male horse who is two years of age or younger.

Conformation. The horse's body structure. This is also referred to as how the horse is "put together." A horse's conformation can help him to be more (or less) suited to various disciplines and activities.

Contact. The connection, through the reins and the bit, between the rider's hands and the horse's mouth, which should be firm but without strain or tension.

Counter-canter. When a horse is purposely ridden on the lead that is opposite to the direction he is going. The counter-canter is used in dressage.

Crest release. Used over jumps, the crest release involves the rider moving her hands evenly up the horse's neck, rising in the stirrups slightly and balancing over the horse's withers to help the horse jump more easily.

Cribbing. When a horse gulps air while biting down on a fence rail or stall door; considered a vice.

Crop. In English riding, a crop is used when the leg aids don't bring about the desired response from the horse or to encourage the horse to greater effort. There are various styles of crops (such as a jumping bat or a dressage whip), but they all perform the same basic function of encouragement or reprimand.

Deworming. Treating a horse for parasites; a necessary component of horse health.

Diagonals. When riding a posting trot, the rider rises slightly in the saddle as the horse's outside shoulder moves forward. When the shoulder moves back, the rider sits. This is called "being on the correct diagonal."

Discipline. A traditional riding style, as in English or Western.

Dressage. Dressage (which is French for "training") consists of complex maneuvers guided by slight cues from the rider.

Drive. Forward impulsion.

Equestrian center. A professional facility that may have multiple arenas, many well-trained horses, and a staff of instructors. Horse shows, exhibitions, and other equestrian-related events are often held here.

Equitation/horsemanship. A type of competition riding that judges the rider's skills and proper positioning, ability to handle the horse, quietness in the saddle, and so on.

Evasion. When the horse refuses to do what the rider asks of him.

Eventing. Also referred to as "three-phase eventing," this is an English discipline that consists of dressage, stadium jumping, and cross-country.

Far side (also **"off side"**). The horse's right side.

Farrier. The person who trims hooves and shoes horses.

Fetlock. The equivalent of a horse's ankle, located on all four legs. This is the joint between the horse's cannon bone (the long bone in the lower leg) and the pastern (the short bone between the fetlock and the horse's hoof).

Filly. A female horse who is two years of age or younger.

Flat work. Riding a horse on the flat means there is no jumping involved in the effort.

Floating teeth. The rasping down of sharp points that develop on a horse's teeth and can interfere with eating and use of the bit.

Foal. A baby horse of either gender.

Gait. The pace at which a horse moves forward. In English, the walk, trot, canter, and gallop; in Western, the walk, jog, lope, and gallop.

Gelding. A castrated male horse of any age.

Girth. The band on an English saddle that goes around the belly to keep the saddle on the horse. Can be made of leather, cotton, or synthetic material and has buckles on each end. (On a Western saddle, the girth is called a "cinch.")

Give. To slightly release tension in the reins, which effectively "gives" to the horse.

Grade horse. A horse without registration papers; often of no particular breed or a cross of two breeds.

Gray. Gray horses can be any shade of gray from white to very dark gray. Most gray horses are born dark and lighten with age.

Green as grass. A class for first-time competitors (either rider or horse).

Grooming. Brushing and combing a horse's or pony's body, mane, and tail, as well as cleaning out their hooves.

Gymkhana. Games on horseback that test the rider's skills and the horse's compliance and training.

Half-halt. A slight pull back on the reins that signals to the horse that a change of activity is coming or that he needs to refocus his attention on the activity at hand.

Halter. Usually made of either leather or nylon, halters are used to catch, lead, and tie horses but should never be left on the horse when he is loose in the pasture or in a stall because of the possibility of it catching on a fence or solid object.

Hands. 1. A horse's or pony's height is measured in hands at the tallest point on the horse's back, his withers. One hand equals four inches. 2. Describes how the rider holds the reins. "Soft hands" (gentle, even contact) is preferred; "hard hands" are too short and tight.

Hard mouth. A horse whose mouth nerves have become insensitive to cues from the bit, usually due to harsh bits and/or bad riders who have hung on the bit or jerked it excessively in the horse's mouth.

Haunches. The hindquarters of a horse or pony.

Hippotherapy. A type of therapy that is facilitated by a professional physical therapist in conjunction with a professional horse handler and volunteers. Sessions are usually private.

Hock. The large, backward-facing joint on a horse's hindleg, which looks much like an elbow on a human.

Impulsion. The energy with which a horse moves forward.

In-hand. When a horse or pony is worked or shown in competition by a handler on foot.

Jog. The gait between a walk and a lope, for Western riders. English riders call this gait the "trot."

Jumping standards. The upright posts between which horizontal poles are placed for jumping.

Leads. When the horse canters, one front leg leads the sequence of footfalls; it strikes the ground slightly ahead of the other front leg. Horses are trained to lead on the inside leg when ridden in a ring; this helps them maintain their balance better. The horse is said to be "on the left (or right) lead" or "on the correct lead."

Leg yield. When the rider applies pressure to the horse's side with one leg and the horse yields to that pressure by moving laterally away from it. This is also an example of the horse "giving" to the rider's "aid."

Lesson barn. Any facility where riding lessons are given.

Loafing shed. A small structure used in pastures to provide shelter to horses from the weather and sun.

Longe (pronounced "lunge"). Working the horse from the ground with a long line attached to the bridle, directing him in a large circle. Longeing ("lunging") is used for a variety of reasons, including simple exercise or warming up, helping a horse release excess energy before a rider mounts, and for training an inexperienced horse.

Lope. In Western riding, the gait between a jog and a gallop. In English riding, this is called the canter.

Mare. A female horse who is three years of age or older.

Mechanical aids. The use of equipment to communicate with the horse. Bridles, bits, reins, saddles, crops (riding whips), and so forth are all examples of mechanical aids.

Mounting block. A stepping stool or block that riders step up onto, which allows them to more easily reach the stirrup and mount a horse.

Near side. The horse's left side.

Neck-reining. A Western style of using the reins against the horse's neck to signal turns, rather than pulling on the bit.

Off side (also **"far side"**). The horse's right side.

On deck. The competitor waiting to go next in the ring is said to be "on deck" and is typically expected to wait in a particular spot.

On the bit. The horse is accepting the bit and the rider's contact.

On the rail. When the horse and rider are moving along in the arena, next to the fence or rail.

Paint/pinto. A horse whose coat consists of solid patches of colored coat and solid patches of white coat. A Paint is a registered breed, while pinto coloring can be found in many different breeds.

Palomino. A horse whose coat is golden and whose mane and tail are white.

Pinto (see **Paint/pinto**).

Pleasure class. A type of competition riding that judges the horse's manners, movement, responsiveness, and way of going; in short, the degree to which the horse appears to be a pleasure to ride.

Poll. The spot on top of a horse's head between his ears.

Pommel. The front of a saddle.

Pony. An equine who is 14.2 hands or shorter.

Post. To rise slightly in the saddle and sit gently in the saddle, in cadence with the horse's trot (see **Diagonals**).

Premium. A guide to scheduled classes that is distributed before a show.

Prospect. A horse that may be suitable for a certain discipline but doesn't yet have the necessary training.

Refusal. When a horse stops in front of an obstacle and refuses to jump.

Riding school. A professional facility that combines a dedicated focus on learning to ride well with hands-on instruction in horse care.

Roan. A horse with an even mixture of white and pigmented hairs that give the coat an overall muted look. A strawberry or red roan has a mix of brown and white hair; a blue roan has black and white hair.

Seat. How the rider sits in the saddle. Having a good seat means having good contact with the horse.

Snip. A small white mark of any shape in the spot between the horse's nostrils.

Sock. A white mark that extends from somewhere around the middle of the cannon bone to the top of the horse's hoof. Any number of legs can have a sock.

Sorrel (see **Chestnut**).

Sound. Healthy, without injury or illness; used to describe both a horse's legs and his wind (breathing capacity).

Stadium jumping. Jumps that are set up in an arena or stadium. These jumps consist of elements that, when struck by the horse, will give or fall down.

Stallion. An intact male horse who is three years of age or older. Young and inexperienced riders should never handle or ride a stallion.

Star. A small white mark, sometimes in a diamond shape, in the center of the horse's forehead.

Stirrup. The piece of equipment that hangs from a saddle, into which the rider's foot is inserted.

Stocking. A white mark that extends from the knee to the top of the horse's hoof. Any number of legs can have a stocking.

Stripe. A long, narrow white stripe that extends down a horse's face from, generally, his forehead to around his muzzle.

Tack. The equipment used for riding a horse; specifically, the bridle, saddle, girth, and saddle pad.

Tacking up. To put the saddle and bridle (the tack) on the horse.

Therapeutic Riding. A type of therapy offered by a professional riding instructor in conjunction with volunteers that often includes a physical, speech, or behavioral therapist as a consultant. Sessions are usually led in groups.

Tie stall. A narrow stall where the horse is haltered and tied; used for feeding and grooming but not suitable for a horse to stay in for long periods of time.

Trot. For English riders, the trot is a two-beat gait, between a walk and a canter. Western riders call this a "jog."

Two-point position. When the rider rises slightly in the saddle, taking her weight in the stirrups, and moves slightly forward in preparation for the horse's propulsion over a jump.

Vices. Undesirable behaviors exhibited by horses; can include cribbing, pawing, kicking at walls, and chewing wood surfaces.

Vintage. Designates a class for riders who are 45 years of age or older.

Withers. The highest point on a horse's back, where the neck and back meet. It is at the withers where a horse's or pony's height is measured.

Helpful Checklists

Here are a few lists to help you identify the right instructor for your child. It's only a starting place, but the following questions should help you well on your way to finding the proper instructor with the right horses for your child. Note that one word you should hear constantly from the instructors you talk with is "safety."

Instructor Checklist

☐ What age riders do you teach?

☐ Are your lesson horses experienced and well-mannered?

☐ What are your teaching qualifications?

☐ What are your safety precautions?

☐ How would you describe your lesson program?

☐ What discipline(s) does your barn specialize in?

☐ Are you a member of any of the equestrian organizations?

☐ Does your barn participate in horse shows?

☐ What is your barn's environment like?

Horse Checklist

☐ Do the horses look healthy, with shiny coats and trim feet?

☐ Do the horses look fit, with slightly rounded bodies and no ribs showing?

☐ Do any of the horses have runny noses, weepy eyes, coughs, or ratty coats?

☐ Are the horses clean and well groomed?

☐ Do the horses calmly obey their handlers and behave quietly?

☐ Do the horses have relaxed expressions or are they pinning their ears and showing the whites of their eyes?

☐ Do the horses have clean water in their stalls, either in buckets or in automatic waterers?

Observations Checklist

As you observe a lesson or two — and even after you've selected a barn for your child to take lessons — there are a number of elements you can observe that will help you assess if a lesson barn or a particular instructor runs a good program with consideration for both riders and horses.

☐ Are all riders wearing hard hats whenever they are on a horse?

☐ Are all riders wearing safe riding boots, with smooth soles and solid heels?

☐ Are all the horses wearing bridles and saddles, or are some horses being ridden bareback with halters only?

☐ Is the tack clean and free of cracks or signs of damage?

☐ Are any of the riders having difficulty with their horses?

☐ If yes, is the instructor prompt in offering calm and positive assistance?

☐ Do handlers interact calmly with the horses or are they loud, sharp with their commands, or using whips excessively?

☐ Do the horses seem to be doing their jobs willingly or are they being difficult?

☐ Do riders seem confident in what the instructor asks them to do and capable of doing it?

☐ Do barn workers seem competent, calm, and capable?

Facilities Checklist

As you walk around during your barn visit and observe a lesson or two — and even after you've selected a barn for your child to take lessons — there are a number of elements you should observe to help ensure the overall safety and maintenance levels observed by the instructor and barn owner.

THE BARN

☐ Are the barn aisles wide enough to accommodate horses passing one another?

☐ If horses are tied in the aisles for grooming and saddling, are the aisles extra wide to allow safe movement past them?

☐ Are the aisles free of clutter or are they used to store hay or tack trunks and other equipment?

☐ Does the barn reek of ammonia and manure?

☐ Do the stalls look clean and relatively free of waste?

☐ Does air seem to move well in the barn or is it stuffy and filled with dust?

☐ Are there lots of birds nesting in the rafters with feces staining everything underneath?

☐ Are there signs of rodents in the tack room and feed storage area?

☐ When stalls are cleaned, is the soiled bedding taken to an appropriate place, far from the barn and riding areas?

☐ Are tools and wheelbarrows neatly put away or left loose and leaning?

☐ Is the tack room neat and tidy?

☐ Are the stall walls and doors secure and well maintained?

☐ Is there a convenient, functional, and tidy bathroom?

THE ARENA

- ☐ Is the arena covered or enclosed?
- ☐ Is the footing smooth and well maintained?
- ☐ Does the footing blow around with the wind and create dust?
- ☐ Are the arena walls or fencing solid and safe with no obstacles or edges jutting out?
- ☐ Is the arena used to store equipment or supplies?
- ☐ Is the arena big enough to accommodate multiple horses safely, even moving at speed?
- ☐ If the arena is outdoor, is it lighted?
- ☐ If it's lighted, are there any shadowy areas or overly bright spots that could confuse a horse or rider?

THE PROPERTY

- ☐ Is the property mowed often enough that the grass doesn't grow excessively long?
- ☐ Do all of the pastures have the things a horse needs to be healthy: space, solid fencing, shade from the sun/shelter from bad weather, and clean water?
- ☐ What is the footing like in the pastures?
- ☐ Do the pastured horses seem healthy and well cared for?
- ☐ If there are aisles between pastures, are they wide enough for horses to be led through without fear of being bitten across a fence?
- ☐ Are the fences in good repair, and are they tall enough and solidly built?

Safe Fencing

Fences are an important part of any equine facility, whether your child is just starting lessons or you are deciding where to board a horse. Use the following questions to make sure the fencing is sturdy and safe.

If fencing is mesh wire:

☐ Is it horse wire with a small weave such that a horse's hoof can't fit through it?

☐ Is the bottom edge buried in the ground?

☐ Is it chain-link fencing, such as you'd see in a backyard? (This is very unsafe for horses.)

If fencing has pipe and cable structure:

☐ Is it smooth and painted?

☐ If rusty, do you see signs of it crumbling and breaking?

☐ If rusty, do you see signs of repairs in progress?

☐ Are the cables taut or are they sagging?

If fencing is electric:

☐ Has wide ribbon-type wire been used?

☐ Is it bare steel electric wire?

☐ If yes, are there flags fluttering along the wire to help with visibility?

☐ Is wire free of breaks, branches lying across it, or overly tall weeds wrapped around it?

☐ Do you hear a quick snapping sound as you walk past certain spots of the wire? (Can indicate a short, making it less effective.)

If fencing is wood:

☐ Are the posts standing upright with the boards firmly fastened to the posts?

☐ Is there an electric wire running along the top rail?

☐ If metal T-posts are used, are there protective plastic caps on the top of every post?

If fencing is vinyl or PVC pipe:

- ☐ Is it used only in areas that do not contain the horses?
- ☐ If containing horses, are the posts and boards strengthened with wood interiors?
- ☐ Are the boards and posts hollow or are they reinforced internally?
- ☐ Is there an electric wire running along the top rail?

If fencing is barbed wire:

- ☐ Is it used only in areas that do not contain horses and places that your child cannot access while riding or handling a horse?
- ☐ Is there any barbed wire lying on the ground anywhere on the property?
- ☐ Are there signs that it is being replaced with other fencing?

Resources for Parents

The following list is by no means exhaustive. Instead, it's intended as a place to start nonequestrian parents in their research. Truly, there is a great deal of support available to you — all you need to know is where to look! Finally, virtually every breed association has a youth element or division, although some are more fully developed, organizationally, than others.

American Youth Horse Council (AYHC)
800-879-2942
www.ayhc.com
The AYHC was established in the early 1970s by breed organizations and Extension specialists to support the youth horse industry. They do this by promoting education, serving as a national information center, and encouraging communications between all breeds and disciplines. The AYHC describes its primary focus as being an advocate for bringing horses and kids together.

National 4-H Council
301-961-2800
www.4husa.org
Serves over 6.5 million members in the United States (aged 5–19) in over 90,000 clubs nationwide. The goal of 4-H is to develop citizenship, leadership, and life skills through mostly agricultural learning programs (including horsemanship), although the 4-H encourages members to learn about many additional topics as well.

NARHA (North American Riding for the Handicapped Association)
800-369-7433
www.narha.org
Since 1969, NARHA has provided Equine Assisted Activity and Therapy (EAAT) programs in the United States and Canada through its network of nearly 800 member centers. Each year, more than 38,000 individuals with disabilities benefit from

activities that include therapeutic riding, hippotherapy, equine-assisted psychotherapy, driving (in a carriage), interactive vaulting (gymnastics on horseback), and competition.

Headquartered in Denver, Colorado, NARHA's mission is to "change and enrich lives by promoting excellence in equine-assisted activities" by ensuring its standards for safety, education, communication, and research are met through an accreditation process for centers and a certification process for instructors.

FEI North American Junior and Young Rider Championships
www.youngriders.org

The premier equestrian competition in North America for junior and young riders, age 14–21, the NAJYRC began in 1974 as an eventing challenge between the United States and Canada. Young equestrians come from the United States, Bermuda, Canada, Mexico, Puerto Rico, and the Caribbean Islands to vie for championships in the three Olympic equestrian disciplines of show jumping, dressage, eventing plus, for the first time in 2008 the Western-style discipline of reining. The competition is run under rules of the FEI (Federation Equestre Internationale, the international governing body for equestrian sport) and is the only FEI championship held in this country.

United States Dressage Federation (USDF)
859-971-2277
www.usdf.org

The United States Dressage Federation is the only national membership organization dedicated to dressage, a method of horse training in existence since ancient Greece and an Olympic sport since the inception of the modern Olympics in the late 1800s. Dedicated to dressage education, recognition of achievement, and promotion of the sport, USDF has more than 30 different educational programs, 125 affiliate local or regional clubs, and more than 2,000 annual awards for excellence in competition.

United States Equestrian Federation (USEF)
859-258-2472
www.usef.org
The national governing body of equestrian sports in the United States. USEF's mission is to regulate equestrian competition with the purpose of ensuring horses' safety and well-being; ensure the enforcement of fair and equitable rules and procedures, up to and including the preparation for the Olympic Games; and improve the level of horsemanship in the United States.

United States Pony Club (USPC)
859-254-7669
www.ponyclub.org
This organization began in the United Kingdom before coming to America in 1954. There are now over 600 clubs across the United States with over 12,000 members. The USPC focuses on teaching children (aged 6–21) to be well-rounded horse people with a thorough knowledge of horses and horse care.

The Official Manual of the Pony Club
This manual is a complete basic guide to horsemanship and horse care in one volume. This is the 13th edition of the worldwide best seller that has helped countless young riders enjoy and succeed in all areas of equitation. No other single volume contains so much information on such a wide range of equestrian topics.

Young Rider **Magazine**
www.youngrider.org
For more than 11 years, *Young Rider Magazine* has taught young people, in an easy-to-read and entertaining way, how to look after their horses properly and how to improve their riding skills safely.

Riding Clothes and Equipment

In addition to local tack stores, there are quite a few online sources for purchasing riding clothes, tack, and horse supplies (like grooming equipment). These sites usually have a "clearance" or "sale" section that would be worth checking before making any purchase. Sometimes, you can find new items at significant savings. If you have any questions, their customer service reps are usually horse people and are excellent resources for helping decide which items to purchase and selecting the proper sizes.

You can shop economically or you can look for the very finest selections — the options are limitless.

Here are a few resources, of the many available:

Dover Saddlery
800-406-8204
www.doversaddlery.com

State Line Tack
800-228-9208
www.statelinetack.com

Breeches USA
866-898-4311
www.breechesusa.com

Manhattan Saddlery
212-673-1400
www.manhattansaddlery.com

The Equestrian Corner
866-908-1082
www.theequestriancorner.com

Acknowledgments

Thank you to Abby for her excitement about this book and her desire to participate. Abby and her pony, Little Bit, served as my models for the art throughout the book, and both were very good-natured about the requests to tilt your head a little this way, now big smile, oops, let's try that again, Little Bit's ears weren't up, okay, here we go, drat, the barn cat got in the way, one more time . . .

Thanks to my husband, Sohail, a city boy who really didn't know what he was getting into when he married a horse-crazy Texan.

To my nonequestrian parents, Bob Gaston and Jeanne McBirney, for not only giving me my first pony but also continuing to support my love of horses, which included everything from physical labor to traveling long distances for horse shows to entertaining my sweet girl when barn duties called me away.

To my brother, Bob Gaston, for a lifetime of love, caring, and steadfast support. You hate horses, but you've gone above and beyond for me: riding the nastiness out of my first pony; suffering through family vacations during which I absolutely HAD to do the trail-riding thing; helping strip stalls after a particularly nasty Virginia winter; taking vacation time to set eight 40-foot metal poles in the ground, trenching and laying electrical wiring, then putting the whole thing together so I could have a lighted arena to ride in at night. For helping yet again by taking more vacation and dragging your wife and four kids to Washington state and working nonstop bush-hogging pastures, tearing down old fences, putting up new ones . . . and for being an unwavering supporter of my crazy idea to write a book. Wow — the list is endless. I love you, bro.

My heartfelt thanks to Mary Sue, for giving up her vacation and for jumping into periodic farm labor with a big smile and a wondrous good will. You're a blessing to my brother and to my family! Thank you Alex, Sam, and Daniel for helping out. I'll never forget Daniel's astonishment at seeing one night's worth of manure in a stall he'd offered to clean out, complete with the querulous, "What have you been feeding these horses?!" And thanks to Caitlin for her frequent visits — just seeing your car in the driveway brightened the day for all of us.

To Tommy Christiansen, many thanks for sharing your beautiful home and property over far too many years to count. You have our immense gratitude, as well, for sharing your expertise, good will, and farm machinery in the early days when we were just getting started.

In appreciation for their interest in this project: Dale Horst of White Oak Ranch in Pilot Point, Texas; Craig Bennight of Falcon Equestrian Center in Terrell, Texas; Shelly Vaughn of Highgate Riding Academy in Heath, Texas. And to the folks at Equest in Wylie, Texas, for the outstanding work you do.

A big thanks goes to Allen and Karen, owners and operators of AKC Services in Quinlan, Texas, for agreeing to meet us late one evening, well after closing hours, so that we could adopt my little girl's first puppy — the sweet, now-enormous yellow Lab, Daisy, who inspired the mention of dogs and horses.

An enormous debt of gratitude to Deb Burns for believing in my idea and to Lisa Hiley, editor extraordinaire. Words can't express my appreciation for your cheerful and skilled guidance. And thank you to Storey Publishing.

Index

Text in *italic* indicates an illustration; text in **bold** indicates a chart.

defined, 70
financial aid for, 66
finding an accredited center, 69,
   71–72
specialized tack and equipment,
   71
therapy horses, 71–72
typical session, *68*
three-phase eventing, 4, 80
tie stall, 130
trail (class with obstacle course), 82
transporting the horse, 100
trot, *56*–58, *57*, 63
   collected trot, 56
   extended trot, 57
   posting or rising trot, 57
   sitting trot, 58
   working trot, 56
trotting posts, 21
turnout, 131, 133
tying a horse, 150, *150*

U

United States Dressage Federation
   (USDF), 20
United States Equestrian
   Federation (USEF), 20
United States Pony Club (USPC),
   20

V

vaccinations, 125, 132
vests
   for shows, 91, 93
   protective, 90
vets, 115, 126–27, 132–33
videotaping your child riding, 54
vintage class, 98
vocalizations, equine, 11–12

W

walk, 54, 62–63
walk/trot classes, 83
water sources, 139
Western disciplines, 4, 28
   barrel racing, 4, 28, 81, *82*
   cutting, 28, 81–82
   pole bending, 82
   ranch horse, 82
   reining, 4, 28, 81

roping, 28, 82
team penning, 4, 82
trail, 82
Western riding, *3*, 3–4
   bridle, 143, *143*
   saddle for beginners, 26
   saddle for shows, 93
Western show attire, 88–94, *90*
   buckles, 92–93
   cowboy boots, *90*, 91
   cowboy hats, 89–90
   glamorous options, 92–93, *93*
   kerchief, 92
   leather belt, 92–93
   protective vests, 90
   riding pants, 91
   shirts, 91
   spurs, 93–94, *94*
Wintec, 151
withers, *5*, 6
World Games, 66, 69

Other Storey Titles You Will Enjoy

Cherry Hill's Horse Care for Kids.
The essentials of equine care, from matching the right horse to the
rider to handling, grooming, feeding, stabling, and much more.
128 pages. Paper. ISBN 978-1-58017-407-7.
Hardcover with jacket. ISBN 978-1-58017-476-3.

Horse Crazy!, by Jessie Haas.
A jam-packed treasure chest of horsey info and
fun for horse-obsessed kids ages 8 and up.
376 pages. Paper. ISBN 978-1-60342-154-6.

Horse Showing for Kids, by Cheryl Kimball.
A one-of-a-kind interactive handbook, filled with checklists and tips
that teach young riders how to have their best show experience.
160 pages. Paper. ISBN 978-1-58017-501-2.
Hardcover with jacket. ISBN 978-1-58017-573-9.

How to Think Like a Horse, by Cherry Hill.
Detailed discussions of how horses think, learn, respond to stimuli, and
interpret human behavior — in short, a light on the equine mind.
192 pages. Paper. ISBN 978-1-58017-835-8.

Jumping for Kids, by Lesley Ward.
A complete program that provides all the fundamentals
of jumping safely and correctly.
144 pages. Paper. ISBN 978-1-58017-672-9.
Hardcover with jacket. ISBN 978-1-58017-671-2.

Judy Richter's Riding for Kids.
A comprehensive handbook to teach young
riders the essentials of horsemanship.
144 pages. Paper. ISBN 978-1-58017-510-4.

These and other books from Storey Publishing are available
wherever quality books are sold or by calling 1-800-441-5700.
Visit us at *www.storey.com*.